COHEN AND TROELTSCH
*Ethical Monotheistic Religion
and Theory of Culture*

Program in Judaic Studies
Brown University
BROWN JUDAIC STUDIES
Edited by
Jacob Neusner,
Wendell S. Dietrich, Ernest S. Frerichs,
Calvin Goldscheider, Alan Zuckerman

Project Editors (Project)

David Blumenthal, Emory University (Approaches to Medieval Judaism)
William Brinner (Studies in Judaism and Islam)
Ernest S. Frerichs, Brown University (Dissertations and Monographs)
Lenn Evan Goodman, University of Hawaii (Studies in Medieval Judaism) (Studies in
Judaism and Islam)
William Scott Green, University of Rochester (Approaches to Ancient Judaism)
Ivan Marcus, Jewish Theological Seminary of America
(Texts and Studies in Medieval Judaism)
Marc L. Raphael, Ohio State University (Approaches to Judaism in Modern Times)
Norbert Samuelson, Temple University (Jewish Philosophy)
Jonathan Z. Smith, University of Chicago (Studia Philonica)

Number 120
COHEN AND TROELTSCH
Ethical Monotheistic Religion
and Theory of Culture
by
Wendell S. Dietrich

COHEN AND TROELTSCH
Ethical Monotheistic Religion and Theory of Culture

by
Wendell S. Dietrich

Scholars Press
Atlanta, Georgia

COHEN AND TROELTSCH
Ethical Monotheistic Religion and Theory of Culture

Library of Congress Cataloging in Publication Data

Dietrich, Wendell S.
  Cohen and Troeltsch : ethical monotheistic religion and theory of culture.

  (Brown Judiac studies ; 120)
  Includes index.
  1. Religion and culture–History of doctrines.
2. Monotheism—History of doctrines.   3. Religion and
ethics—History of doctrines. 4. Cohen, Hermann,
1842-1918. 5. Troeltsch, Ernest, 1865-1923. I. Title.
II. Series.
BL65.C8D54   1986   291.1'7   86-6577
ISBN 1-55540-017-5 (alk. paper)
ISBN 1-55540-018-3 (pbk. : alk. paper)

Printed in the United States of America
on acid-free paper

For Sarah and John

CONTENTS

Preface

One of the most exciting items on the current intellectual scene is the renewed interest in Ernst Troeltsch's thought. American, British, German, and French scholars are concurrently forwarding that renewal. Equally exciting is the revival of interest in Hermann Cohen's thought. And once again it is an international cohort—American, German, French, and Israeli—who share in that enthusiasm.

My interest in Troeltsch is a longstanding one. Professor H. Richard Niebuhr, my principal mentor at Yale University Graduate School, was the one who first taught me to take Troeltsch seriously. And the reading of Troeltsch in this monograph owes much to careful study over the years of Professor Niebuhr's *Radical Monotheism and Western Culture* (New York: Harper and Bros., 1960). My understanding of Troeltsch as a theorist of culture was also stimulated by another Yale mentor, Professor Hans Frei. Continued discussion of Troeltsch with colleagues in the Nineteenth Century Theology Working Group of the American Academy of Religion has been an invaluable resource for me.

My interest in the thought of Hermann Cohen and in modern Judaic thought is of somewhat more recent vintage. I have had special impetus to venture into the study of modern Judaic thought since 1969: it was at that point that I began to work with and be instructed by the splendid group of graduate students brought to Brown by our doctoral program in Judaism in Late Antiquity under the direction of Professor Jacob Neusner.

I have recently conducted seminars in the Brown Program in Judaic Studies on "Mendelssohn, Cohen and Rosenzweig," and my scholarly interests in Hermann Cohen first found published statement in an article on "The Function of the Idea of Messianic Mankind in Hermann Cohen's Later Thought" (*Journal of the American Academy of Religion* 48 [1980]: 245-258). This tyro's effort was greeted with extraordinary generosity by my friend Professor Steven Schwarzschild of the Philosophy Department of Washington University, an editor of the new German critical edition of Cohen's *Werke*, to whom I am deeply indebted. (I was also much encouraged by a thoughtful critical appraisal of that article by Professor Edith Wyschogrod.)

Professor Schwarzschild and I have continued our exchanges on Cohen. I was honored to appear with him in December 1982 at an American Academy of Religion session of the History of Judaism Section, History of Jewish Philosophy Subsection, on "The Intellectual Sources of the Thought of

Hermann Cohen." The topic of my own paper was "Hermann Cohen's Objections to Ernst Troeltsch's Interpretation of the Prophetic Ethos." Once again Professor Schwarzschild's generous but rigorous response was encouraging.

My interpretation of Cohen has been continually sharpened by subsequent exchanges among colleagues in the History of Jewish Philosophy Subsection of the History of Judaism Section of the American Academy of Religion.

My interest in the comparative study of the major modern systems of Christian and Judaic thought has been stimulated by teaching assignments in both the Department of Religious Studies and the Program in Judaic Studies at Brown University. I also had an opportunity to think some of these issues through for the first time during two happy terms in 1981 as a Visiting Professor of Religion at Dartmouth College.

In the preparation of this monograph, I have ventured to hope that those interested in recovering the heritage of Ernst Troeltsch as interpreter of the Christian ethos and as systematic religious thinker also can be persuaded to take seriously some concerns that Troeltsch himself took very seriously: the debates between the Southwest Baden School of neo-Kantianism to which he adhered and the Marburg School of neo-Kantianism headed by Hermann Cohen, and the attempts by a modern Jewish philosopher of religion like Cohen to reconstruct Judaic thought as ethical monotheism. I also hope that historians of modern Jewish thought can be persuaded to take seriously the exchange between a figure like Hermann Cohen and a Christian debating partner like Troeltsch. (In this respect, I owe more than I can say to the work of the late Professor Uriel Tal of Tel Aviv who always expressed toward me an unfailing courtesy and interest.)

We are past the time when historians of nineteenth- and twentieth-century Christian and Judaic thought can work in hermetically sealed compartments.

I hope that what I have to say here may be of modest interest as well to interpreters of the Hebrew Bible and historians of the modern interpretation of the Old Testament. Admittedly neither Cohen nor Troeltsch is a biblical scholar, but they know the literature and look deeply into the issues. What they do with what they learn is an important part of my story here.

This monograph permits me to bring to extended statement a set of long-standing interests. I am grateful to the current chairman of the Brown Department of Religious Studies, Professor John P. Reeder, Jr., for his encouragement of my scholarly work. Professor Jacob Neusner with whom I serve as a professor of Judaic Studies at Brown has constantly stirred me to high ambitions and judged my work with both rigor and generosity.

My wife Betsy typed early drafts of this monograph. She has unfailingly encouraged me to believe I had scholarly contributions to make.

In this monograph I bring contributions from past generations to the present.

And I believe those contributions are resources for the future. That is why I dedicate the monograph to my children, Sarah and John.

Funds for the production of this book were provided from a gift to the Brown Program in Judaic Studies in honor of the late Max Richter by Mr. Nathan Abrams of New York. This aid is gratefully acknowledged.

Lila Weinberg contributed her remarkable resources of intelligence and sound judgment to the editing of this book. I am much in her debt.

Introduction

This monograph presents two late nineteenth-century proposals for the reconstruction of classic Western religious traditions. One proposal, Hermann Cohen's, is for the revision of classic Judaism; the other, Ernst Troeltsch's, is for the revision of Western Christianity. Both proposals recommend reinterpreting their respective classical traditions as ethical monotheisms.

That means a religious concentration and intensity that focuses singular attention on God in contrast to all creaturely reality; it also means, in a modern world in process of secularization, describing and interpreting religion as the expression of human powers crystallized in discrete and distinct symbols, texts, and institutions. Nonetheless these two proposals for ethical monotheism do not recommend withdrawal from the world of social and cultural life. Both display an inclusive interest in culture and society and insist that ethical monotheistic faith energizes the construction of culture.

In Chapter I of this monograph I present the constructive proposals of both Hermann Cohen and Ernst Troeltsch for the reinterpretation of Judaism and Christianity, respectively, as ethical monotheistic religion. In Chapter IV, I set out their respective ethical monotheistic theories of culture and society.

Clearly there are striking similarities and convergences between their proposals. But there are also critical differences. Chapters II and III focus especially on these differences and probe for the grounds of the divergence.

In Chapter II, I treat "the prophetic ethos in dispute." Both Cohen and Troeltsch regard the prophetic faith and ethos as a principal resource for the contemporary reconstruction of ethical monotheism. For Cohen the prophetic faith and ethos constitute an unsurpassable moment in the religion of Judaism, the normative resource for the construction of a religion of reason out of the sources of Judaism. Troeltsch judges the "prophetic principle" to be a crucial element in his theological system; and for Troeltsch, the Christian theologian, the normative original point at which faith in the one God is mediated by the Christ to the whole of humanity can only be properly interpreted in relation to the prophetic faith in the one transcendent God, the governor of human history and destiny. Moreover, Troeltsch, not surprisingly, but also Cohen, unexpectedly for a Judaic thinker, both employ the results of modern historical critical interpretation of the prophets. Cohen, however, aligning himself with the Wellhausen generation of Old Testament scholarship, reads the prophets as advocates of eternally valid principles for the organization of a just, egalitarian society. Troeltsch vigorously rejects such an interpretation of the prophets.

1

Aligning himself with Weber and new perspectives that see religious beliefs and social ethical views as conditioned by and expressions of a social situation, Troeltsch insists upon the "utopian" character of prophetic politics. The prophets, according to Troeltsch, espouse, within the world of urban life in the post-Davidic monarchies, the simpler norms of clan-brotherliness from an earlier epoch. In advocating these norms, the prophets challenge any endorsement of the conditions and norms of urban life; and they protest against Israel caving in to what are taken to be the inevitable trends and dynamisms of great power politics. On the basis of this construing of the prophetic ethos, Troeltsch provocatively claims for the prophets not an ascetic other-worldliness but a "relative indifference to the construction of culture." Cohen sharply disputes such a reading of the prophets. Happily enough, there is major documentation for this controversy between Cohen and Troeltsch, the exposition of which is the topic of Chapter II.

Though the ostensible topic of the controversy recounted in Chapter II is the proper interpretation and legitimate contemporary appropriation of the prophetic faith and ethos, other factors are obviously at play in the dispute. Most significant are differences between Cohen and Troeltsch that emerge out of Cohen's adherence to the Marburg school of neo-Kantianism and Troeltsch's adherence to the Southwest Baden school of neo-Kantianism which, with its concern for method in history, exhibits neo-Hegelian as well as neo-Kantian themes and procedures.

Such divergences between two rival schools of neo-Kantianism as exemplified by Cohen and Troeltsch also come to the fore in Chapter III, where the distinctive character of Cohen's regulative social ideal is highlighted by describing it in the context of charges by Cohen's opponents in the rival neo-Kantian school—charges that Cohen's social ethic is yet another instance of that empty and abstract formalism which, Cohen's opponents allege, is the typical defect of Marburg neo-Kantianism. Cohen's social ethic is a theory of that Enlightenment and post-Enlightenment society which sees as its principal reason for being the continuing emancipation of man. In this chapter also I present Troeltsch as a social philosopher and ethicist who seeks to recast the Christian ethic in a modern idiom. In executing that project, Troeltsch employs the conceptions both of a neo-Kantian ethic of conviction and a neo-Hegelian objective ethic of values instantiated in the structures of institutions and ethos. Moreover, the presentation of the social ethic of Cohen and Troeltsch in Chapter III precipitates for investigation a further set of considerations: Is there a distinctive compatability between Kantian modes of philosophizing and the Judaic religious tradition? Is there a Judaic as well as a Marburg neo-Kantian component in Cohen's antagonism to Troeltsch's neo-Hegelian philosophizing? Is there an affinity between neo-Hegelian patterns of thought and Troeltsch's commitments as a Christian social philosopher?

In sum, I set out in this monograph Cohen's and Troeltsch's constructive proposals for reinterpreting their respective religious traditions as ethical monotheistic religion (Chapter I) and their correlative ethical monotheistic theories of culture and society (Chapter IV). But the more precise interpretation and appraisal of the differences as well as similarities between Cohen and Troeltsch require an investigation of the prophetic ethos in dispute (Chapter II) and the grounds for divergence: neo-Kantian and neo-Hegelian orientations in social ethics (Chapter III).

Chapter 1

MONOTHEISTIC RELIGION: CONSTRUCTIVE PROPOSALS BY COHEN AND TROELTSCH

Two major proposals emerge on the late nineteenth-century German religious and intellectual scene—proposals for revising classic Western religious traditions in the interests of enhancing their credibility in the modern world. Both proposals recommend ethical monotheism as the credible form of modern religion and as a suitable base for modern culture. One of these proposals is a revision of Classic Judaism. Its proponent is the Marburg neo-Kantian moral philosopher, Hermann Cohen. The other proposal is a revision of the Western Christian tradition. Its proponent is the Heidelberg neo-Kantian and neo-Hegelian religious thinker and interpreter of the Christian ethos, Ernst Troeltsch.

It is characteristic of both these proposals that they forecast a certain convergence between Judaism and Christianity. Moreover, each thinker works out his proposal with the alternative Western religious tradition specifically in view. And, happily for the purposes of this investigation, in the case of Cohen and of Troeltsch each has the work of the other in mind in setting out his own proposal. Cohen takes Troeltsch's views into account as part of the neo-Ritschlian Protestantism with which Cohen is generally sympathetic. Troeltsch for his part carefully appraises Cohen's religion of reason out of the sources of Judaism. Indeed, Cohen's is the sole contemporary version of Judaic religious philosophy that Troeltsch treats in any detail.

Yet, in the midst of convergence, profound and pervasive differences between Cohen and Troeltsch emerge. Cohen believes without qualification that a reconstructed Judaism and not Christianity is the most suitable base for modern culture. He resists the co-opting of Judaism as a secondary element in a Judeo-Christian tradition. Troeltsch, no doubt, is sympathetic with the "Hebraic" element in the Western tradition. Indeed his Christian ethical monotheism is a prophetic ethical monotheism. But, though Troeltsch harbors no strong hostility toward Judaism and engages Cohen in respectful debate, Troeltsch cannot imagine any other religion than Christianity playing the principal role in the Western "culture circle." No doubt Troeltsch, in his theory of society and culture, rejects a "Christian state" that appeals, in general public life, to specifically Christian warrants for the state's authority and operation. In fact, Troeltsch edges close to the notion of a religiously pluralist society. But it

5

never occurs to him to assign to Judaism a significant role in modern culture.

The proposals of Cohen and Troeltsch, in their theoretical conceptual elaboration and in their cultural and societal ramifications, are set out in a body of literature produced principally in the second decade of the twentieth century. Cohen, after his retirement in 1912 from the chair of philosophy at Marburg which he had occupied since 1876, began to lecture at the "Hochschule fuer die Wissenschaft des Judentums" in Berlin. In those lectures on "The Concept of Religion in the System of Philosophy" (Cohen, 1915), Cohen turns, in a way previously unprecedented, to the theme of religion. His treatment nonetheless is entirely consistent with his previous system of philosophy which already encompasses logic, epistemology, ethics, esthetics, and theory of culture. During this same period, Cohen's adherence to the German political and cultural cause in World War I provokes his most extended reflections on the compatibility of Judaism and the modern spirit in its German form (1914). During this final period of his authorship, Cohen also produces his "Religion of Reason out of the Sources of Judaism" (1929; English translation 1972), posthumously published in 1919. This major systematic work along with the essay on the "Concept of Religion" provides the principal systematic statement of Cohen's ethical monotheism. My exposition of Cohen in this monograph is drawn from the literature of this final period in Cohen's authorship.

Troeltsch works out his version of ethical monotheism in the latter phase of the middle period of his authorship, during the concluding days of his tenure as professor of theology at Heidelberg and during the early days of his tenure as professor in the Philosophical Faculty in Berlin. A key statement of Troeltsch's ethical monotheism is to be found in his *Glaubenslehre*, his systematic theological lectures at Heidelberg in 1911 and 1912 (1925c). Since these lectures were published only posthumously in 1925, it would be inaccurate to suppose they were available earlier than that to the general learned public or available at all to Cohen. But the *Glaubenslehre* in fact states systematically and with greater fullness, cogency, and detail what Troeltsch argues in works published between 1912 and 1918. Of such published works, two are crucial: the classic essay in 1916 on "The Faith and Ethos of the Hebrew Prophets" (1925a), and its 1917 companion piece on the faith and ethos of primitive Christianity and the Ancient Catholic Church, "Die alte Kirche" (1925b).

During this same period, Troeltsch takes careful note of Cohen's work, reviewing Cohen's book on the "Concept of Religion" (Troeltsch, 1918) and a pamphlet of Cohen's on the "Religious Movements of the Present" (Troeltsch, 1915). Moreover, Troeltsch's essay on "The Faith and Ethos of the Hebrew Prophets" provokes in 1917 an impassioned reply by Cohen, "Der Prophetismus und die Soziologie" (Cohen, 1917a).

In this initial chapter, I shall set out Cohen's and Troeltsch's alternative versions of ethical monotheism as a conceptual system. In each case, I shall note first methods of procedure and how each thinker proposes to employ the sources of his tradition. I shall then indicate in each instance the principal assertions of ethical monotheism as a pattern of belief.

Cohen's version of ethical monotheism is in some respects typical of many such attempts by nineteenth-century Judaic thinkers to recast Judaism as ethical monotheism. But Cohen's proposal is noteworthy not only for its fullness and range but also for its methodological sophistication. As one might expect of a neo-Kantian, precision of method is a heavy preoccupation of the "Concept of Religion" (1915) and the "Religion of Reason" (1929). To speak technically, Cohen employs a "method of correlation," a method for exhibiting the mutual implication of concepts in a total postulatory philosophical scheme. But Cohen's neo-Kantianism is not a constricted reduction of philosophy to theory about method in the various sciences: natural, historical, and moral. The "method of correlation" culminates in the notion of the "correlation of God and man." The "idea of God" plays a decisive and controlling role in the whole system of postulates.

Among present-day interpreters, it is Alexander Altmann (1962) who has, in my judgment, correctly interpreted Cohen and his method of correlation. In my presentation, I find with Altmann at every critical controversial juncture, against alternative views.

For Cohen's total scheme, the point of departure is logic. Cohen's logic is not classic formal logic but the Marburg neo-Kantian "logic of origination" which begins with "origin" (*Ursprung*) in the mathematical context of the infinitesimal calculus. Here the concept of "correlation" is first employed (Altmann, 1962: 379, 383, 384). Here a basic pattern is set for exhibiting the reciprocal relation and mutual implication of concepts. Through this "correlation" of concepts, the System of Philosophy is constructed.

From the logical, the construction of the scheme moves to spatial relations and the concept of correlation functions there, but still in a totally immanent way (Altmann, 1962: 384, 385). In the next phase of constructing the scheme, purpose (*Zweck*) comes into view, and correlation functions as a concept of purpose (Altmann, 1962: 381). Such a notion of purpose is not the popular one in which a multiplicity of means are related to a controlling and superordinating end. Rather Cohen focuses once again on the mutual reciprocity of concepts in the system. Purpose looks back toward, complements, and interacts with "origin."

But with the introduction of purpose into the scheme, there is movement forward to the moral life of man and its postulates. The idea of God comes on the scene in the moral sphere and the way is open toward the sphere of religion, in its distinctiveness from, but never its independence of, ethics. The definitive religious notion is the correlation of God and man.

In his ethical writings, prior to the final phase of his authorship, Cohen introduces the concept of God as a postulate of the moral life. It is only in the "Concept of Religion" and the "Religion of Reason," however, that the scheme is worked out in its totality and the full range of meanings of the concept of God in the context of ethical monotheism is displayed.

Once again the matter is technically stated through the notion of the correlation of God and man. The fundamental methodological notion of correlation takes on new meanings, according to Cohen, when one takes into account data from religious life and the sources of Judaism. Correlation is not simply a logical but a metalogical concept used in the context of a distinctively religious notion of the correlation of God and man (Altmann, 1962: 383-386, 397). This metalogical usage of correlation is Cohen's way of handling the classic problem of predication with respect to the divine being. Cohen, in line with his reading of the classic tradition of Medieval Jewish philosophy, treats the divine attributes as attributes of action. At this juncture, and I refer here to the initial formulations in the "Concept of Religion" and the extensive exposition in the "Religion of Reason," Cohen adduces the religious-theological notion of God the Creator and the world in its totality as creaturely, though it is still man in the context of nature who is principally denominated creature. Thus, in this metalogical use of the concept of correlation, one is permitted to speak of the creaturely world and its preservation and to gather up what has previously been stated about nature and man initially under the rubric of the logical category of origination (*Ursprung*) and subsequently under the rubric of purpose (*Zweck*).

Employing the correlation Creator-creature thus has the surprising result of propelling Cohen's neo-Kantian system in a new direction. Within the sphere of ethics and the ethical function of the idea of God, Cohen refers to nature principally as the area of moral activity and to God as the guarantor of that area. In the new setting, nature becomes creation. Cohen also refers in this context, in a new way, to the becoming of nature and the being of God. But, let there be no mistake, Cohen does not, as Rosenzweig erroneously claimed, make a move to actuality, a breakthrough to an ontological system. Cohen's is still a postulatory system in which ideas, including the idea of God, function as hypotheses. Cohen's is a post-Kantian version of the Platonic tradition of classical philosophy.

Even though nature thus can become, in the distinctiveness of its religious placement, creation, the focus of the system is still on man as creature. For the exhibition of this point, the opening sections of the "Religion of Reason" are crucial. The concepts of origination and purpose drive toward the theme of knowledge. The religious transposition of these concepts drives to the notion of revelation reinterpreted as "creation in reason." The notion of spirit, with its connotations from the biblical understanding of man and from idealistic philosophies, is specified as a mediating concept, pointing to the correlation of God and man (Altmann, 1962: 385, 386).

Cohen's system thus moves from the logic of origination to metalogical considerations of the correlation of God and creation. In a parallel fashion, meanings expressed in the ethical sphere in a purposive notion of correlation now come into reciprocal relation with the religious concept of redemption (*Erloesung*) from sin. A metaethical correlation emerges. Here the religious is normatively exhibited as distinct from, but not in contradiction to, the ethical. In the ethical sphere, the God-idea functions to guarantee the eternity of the ethical ideal as well as the eternal preservation of nature as the arena for ethical activity (Altmann, 1962: 386). The eternal ethical task is the construction of humanity. The moral life, thus construed, is concerned with man in the totality (*Allheit*) of humanity, not with the individual. On the other hand, for Cohen "the conceptual origin of religion lies in the consciousness of sin of the individual" (Altmann, 1962: 386). This claim is not at all an assertion in the field of the history of religions about empirically identifiable "origins of religion" in the past. Nor, to turn to the religion that most interests Cohen, is this claim a descriptive characterization of the totality of the classic sources of Judaism nor an account of Judaism's development. In the strictest sense, the claim is a statement about the mutual implication of concepts in the purified scheme of Judaic ethical monotheism that Cohen wishes to commend.

Cohen deals with these issues systematically in the "Concept of Religion." In the "Religion of Reason," the exposition is filled out in more detail as systematic claims are coordinated with the derivation of concepts from the sources of Judaism, especially the early writing prophets and the Deuteronomic teaching. It should be noted that although "the conceptual origin of religion lies in the consciousness of the sin of the individual," Cohen builds slowly and carefully toward a treatment of the individual starting with interhuman relations. According to Cohen, a man who is merely contiguous to another (*Nebenmensch*) becomes a fellowman only through sympathy (Altmann, 1962: 388). The most dramatic exemplary instance of sympathy is sympathy with the suffering of the impoverished. Here we have Cohen's neo-Kantian socialist reading of the prophets. A key test and limit case for this recognition of the fellowman is the attitude toward the alien in one's midst.

Thus the groundwork for the correlation of man and God, Cohen insists, is the correlation of man with man as fellowman "before God." On the basis of this sympathetic love of man for fellowman before God, one takes the next step. One may point, in terms of the attributes of divine action, to God's love for man. However, this notion is not, I take it, fundamental and constitutive in Cohen's scheme.

Within this complex of relations, one can at last also speak of the correlation between the unique God and the unique man, the "absolute individual." This "absolute individual" is recognized as the individual acknowledges a consciousness of sin and of God as Redeemer from sin. In a fashion entirely consistent with his postulatory scheme of meanings for the idea of God, Cohen does not speak of a divine act, a divine declaration of forgiveness. Rather man repents "before" the transcendent God who guarantees the meaningfulness of repentance (*Sinnhaftigkeit der Busse*). This is the liberating of man, a pledge of the ultimate success of ethical endeavor (Altmann, 1962: 386).

In the strictest sense, these aspects of the correlation of God and man thus far adduced constitute Judaic religion as ethical monotheism. But there is one final dimension of the correlation of God and man, the metaesthetic. Cohen, in characterizing man, uses the notion of correlation in a metalogical context, moving the problem of knowledge into the realm of revelation as "creation in reason" and "spirit." He uses the notion of correlation in a metaethical context, connecting moral activity with the realm of redemption. Correlation as a concept and the correlation of God and man also has a metaesthetic dimension. The correlation of God and man has ramifications in the sphere of man's desire (Altmann, 1962: 394-397). Here Cohen, especially in the "Concept of Religion" but also in the exposition in the "Religion of Reason" of the "nearness of God," treats religion as feeling. In the "Concept of Religion," he engages in extensive debate with Schleiermacher and Spinoza. Cohen's basic preoccupation is with an iconoclastic ethical monotheistic attack on the tendency to conflate religious and esthetic feeling. Religious feeling properly construed is not merely longing for the infinite, a pantheistic affirmation of the All. Rather man the creature must acknowledge his finitude before God. Only with these reservations registered is it appropriate to speak of man's love for God, the individual's yearning for God, and, with the psalmist, the nearness of God. This nearness of God at last provides comfort in the midst of man's innocent suffering.

Thus Cohen spells out the correlation of God and man as a pattern of meanings which starts with the metalogical employment of the idea of God the Creator, then moves to the metaethical idea of God the Redeemer, and finally moves to the metaesthetic employment of the idea of God as focus for man's yearning and love. In some respects this may appear a self-enclosed system which never breaks beyond the "idea of God." But, in my judgment, precisely in the way Cohen combats the erroneous conflation of esthetic and religious feeling, precisely in his insistence on man's finitude before God, the center of gravity is God. This is Judaic monotheism.

Cohen presents ethical monotheism as a scheme of meanings, a postulatory scheme in which the idea of God functions in certain ways. But, as I have already noted, that scheme of meanings is filled out in a specific way when data is brought into the scheme from religious life and from the sources of Judaism.

That means that the religion of reason Cohen wishes to commend is a properly purified and reconceived Judaism. Such a reconceived Judaism can be, Cohen insists, derived from the sources of Judaism. What is at stake in such a derivation, and what sources does Cohen have in view?

The sources from which this religion of reason is derived are principally biblical ("Old Testament") sources, as those biblical sources are read in conjunction with classic Rabbinic tradition and the philosophical tradition of medieval Jewish thought. To use classic Judaic categories, the Bible as "Written Torah" is read through the filter of and in connection with the "Oral Torah" of Rabbinic tradition and medieval philosophy.

Cohen then is not a "Biblicist" who reduces Judaism to a single source, the biblical. Nonetheless Cohen does hold that the whole of Judaism as a religion of reason can be derived from the biblical sources. That does not mean that the whole content of Judaism as a religion of reason present in the Bible is present there conceptually articulated. In fact, the classic culture of Judaism with its exclusive monotheistic religious preoccupation has little proclivity for philosophy. Philosophy as such, Cohen unabashedly contends, is the creation of the Greek spirit. In the Bible, a religion is to be found in literary forms especially suited to religious expression and formulated in a manner essentially different from philosophy or a system of philosophy. But that which is present in the Bible in literary form is susceptible of conceptual articulation, and processes are already underway in the Bible which prompt and invite that further articulation. (Proper understanding of Cohen's derivation of a religion of reason from the biblical sources can best be gained in connection with the argument of Eliezer Schweid [1983] in a recent essay on Cohen as a biblical exegete. I am indebted to Howard Eilberg-Schwartz, a student in my 1984 graduate seminar on Cohen, who brought to the attention of the seminar the details of Schweid's essay, an essay unhappily not yet available in English translation.)

It is modern biblical criticism, Cohen contends, that permits one to discern processes underway, in the biblical period and registered in the biblical document, which prompt and invite further articulation. Moreover, modern biblical criticism helps to set the agenda for Cohen's own systematization and "idealization" of Judaism as a religion of reason. To thus exploit biblical criticism is a bold and daring move, hitherto unprecedented in Judaic thought. Making that move not only gives Cohen an advantage in his apologia for Judaism: Judaism can be defended by recourse to the most advanced results of critical scholarship. It also provides an invigorating impetus to the construction of his system.

Cohen unhesitatingly takes over the apparatus and major results of Wellhausen's historical critical reading of the Old Testament (Cohen, 1918). Cohen of course rejects Wellhausen's claim, still so much in line with the older Christian notions of a Christian supersession of a moribund first-century Judaism, that only primitive Christianity renews the prophetic spirit in the first century. Cohen does accept Wellhausen's notion that the second, prophetic, phase of the religion of Israel transformed a vital but diffusely focused early cultic religion into universal monotheism oriented toward history and the messianic future. For Cohen, this prophetic phase is religiously unsurpassable. He accepts with reservations but assesses differently Wellhausen's treatment of postexilic "early Judaism" with its focus on law, the operation of the central sacrificial cultus, and the protection of ethnic identity. Such developments are for Cohen, in disagreement with Wellhausen, not simply a falling away from the prophetic achievement. They are rather necessary developments in shaping the identity of the "congregation of the people Israel."

The Bible, when it is read critically, is the source of data for a proper reconstruction of the history of the religion of Israel. But the Bible as a literary document also commands attention. The various products of these phases of the religion of Israel are deposited in literary form in the books of the Bible in their final redaction. Diverse blocks of material, reflecting differing stages of religious consciousness, are juxtaposed as the biblical books are given shape and transmitted. Redactors edit and revise these diverse materials, especially the Pentateuchal books of Genesis, Exodus, and Deuteronomy. And, astonishingly enough, the evidence of this reworking is available for all to see. This produces a tension which compels the mind to reflect. The religious literature of the Bible invites the process of conceptual articulation, systematization, and "idealization" according to a norm.

With respect to content, Cohen himself carries out the process of idealization with prophetic religion as the norm. He believes there are warrants in the Bible itself for such a procedure. The normative center of biblical literature, Cohen contends, is the books of the writing prophets. The legal materials of the Pentateuch are redacted, Cohen asserts following the Wellhausen school, under the impact of prophetic religion. Exemplary in this connection is the book of Deuteronomy, the definitive commentary on all the mythic, epic narrative, and legal materials to be found in the Pentateuch as a whole. In Deuteronomy's version of the giving of the Torah, mythical elements found in the Exodus account are deleted. In Deuteronomy, the stress of Exodus on God as a ruler interested in exacting retribution is corrected by a stress on the indissolubility of God's justice and mercy. Whereas Exodus portrays the truth as being externally communicated, according to Deuteronomy truth is in the heart. This sort of revision of biblical materials interior to the canon invites and provokes that critical reflection which issues both in "idealization" according to an ethical monotheistic norm and systematization.

Cohen's proposal for the revision of Judaism as ethical monotheism can be understood then by focusing on his method of correlation and on how the idea of God is employed in the totality of the scheme, especially when that idea is filled out with data from the sources of Judaism. Such investigation further leads, as I have indicated, to consideration of what, in the technical sense, it means to derive a religion of reason from the sources of Judaism.

Cohen interprets Judaism in a rigourous technical sense as monotheistic religion. To call Judaism a religion is currently so common that it is hard to credit the fact that such an interpretation is a nineteenth-century invention. Classic Rabbinic Judaism, it is clear, is a system of life and thought in which ritual, culture, and ethnic identity are interconnected and inseparable. Rabbinic Judaism is not classically presented as simply one distinctive sphere of human activity and consciousness, the religious, alongside others. The notion of Judaism as religion can emerge only when Enlightenment thinkers produce a notion of religion as one among multiple expressions of human powers, and when emancipated Jews begin to function as religious individuals in religious associations in early modern European society. In the specific context of life in nineteenth-century Germany, to say Judaism is a religion means that Judaism is a religious "confession" comparable to Roman Catholicism and Protestantism.

The issue is further complicated by the fact that the first great theorist of emancipated Judaism, Moses Mendelssohn, calls Judaism not a "revealed religion" but rather "revealed legislation." Mankind generally, Mendelssohn contends in *Jerusalem* (1783), can recognize the universal truths of religion which are identical with the metaphysical truths of reason: the existence of God, providence, and the immortality of the soul. The properly observant Jew further takes into account, in addition to these universal truths of reason, certain truths of historical fact: the sacred history of Exodus and Sinai. The observant Jew, according to Mendelssohn, also recognizes that at Sinai God revealed a body of ritual legislation especially intended for the Jewish people.

The terms for Cohen's discussion at the end of the nineteenth century are set by Mendelssohn's initial formulation. The problem is deepened by the fact that Kant adopts, in *Religion within the Limits of Reason Alone*, Mendelssohn's characterization of Judaism. That means for Kant that Judaism is merely a "statutory religion." Ecclesiastical Christianity, not Judaism, according to Kant, is the historical matrix out of which rational, ethical religion can emerge in the modern West (Cohen, 1929: 415, 416; 1972: 357, 358).

Cohen confronts head-on Mendelssohn's setting of the debate's terms and Kant's dismissal of Judaism. He also takes into account the situation in German society in which Gentiles in general and official institutions in particular interpret Judaism as a religious confession. Moreover, Cohen notes that, interior to developing nineteenth-century Judaic life, the Reform movement interprets Judaism as a religion, divesting it of particular national identity. This is the background of Cohen's own vindication of Judaic ethical monotheism as a religion of reason. Such a religion can meet the standards of validity set by universal human reason. Such a religion does not contradict but is compatible with the universal autonomous moral consciousness. But such a religion, according to Cohen, does not neglect the fact that religion emerges in a particular matrix, employing traditional sources.

Cohen's interpretation of Judaism as monotheistic religion is informed by yet another factor. He knows that historians of religion are impressing the learned public more and more with the plurality and variety of religion. His own discussion is colored by that. Cohen is fully alert to change and development in religion, especially in the religion of Ancient Israel. He embraces the results of a critical reconstruction of the history of Israel's developing religion. On the other hand, he asserts, it is finally incumbent on the religious thinker, aware of the plurality of data, to stipulate the normative meaning of the concept of religion and to indicate where such religion is exemplified.

Cohen's interpretation of Judaism as religion also shows the impact of the late nineteenth-century German Protestant theological tendency to identify religion with the individual. Cohen's Marburg neo-Kantian Ritschlian colleague, Wilhelm Herrmann, had complained that Cohen, though employing the idea of God in his major ethical writings, has little to say about the religious individual. In the face of this Ritschlian Protestant critique, Cohen puts forward in the "Concept of Religion" (1915) his own concept of the absolute individual in correlation with the unique God. This individual sanctifies himself "before God." This is a characteristically Judaic and indeed Rabbinic formulation. Moreover, Cohen warrants his distinctive view of the religious individual from the sources of Judaism by giving special attention to Ezekiel, the exilic prophet who moves beyond the consensus of the early writing prophets with their focus on social justice. Ezekiel stresses the individual, his guilt and responsibility, and also calls for a reconstituted cult as an instrument of sanctification. The distinctive piety of the individual in the Bible, Cohen contends, is also expressed in the literary form of the lyric of the psalms. One may conclude then that, for Cohen, the Protestant theologian Herrmann is both a partner and an adversary. Herrmann compels Cohen to focus on the religious individual, but Cohen produces a distinctively Judaic view, warranted from the Bible, deliberately set in contrast with the Pauline, Augustinian, Lutheran Christian picture of the religious individual.

Moreover, though Judaic religion deals with the individual's consciousness of guilt, Judaic religion is never solely a matter of the individual. It is exactly in this context that Cohen's treatment of the relation of the religious and the ethnic is so fascinating. In the "Religion of Reason," Cohen works the matter out with great conceptual rigor as he argues for the mutual implication and correlation of the concepts of religion and nationality (*Nationalitaet*).

Judaism, Cohen insists, affirms the one God as universal Lord of all the nations and their history. But Judaism also indispensably has what Cohen chooses to call, in nineteenth-century language, a dimension of nationality. (In current idiom, I should call it an ethnic dimension.) The pertinent category, Cohen insists, is nationality, not nation. The way the notion is worked out makes it clear that Cohen's notion of nationality cannot be assimilated to the problem of nationalities or Jewry as nationality as that question is being debated in Cohen's time in Southern and Central Europe or in the Russian territories. Moreover, Cohen specifically contests the Zionist equation of Jewish nationality and Jewish nation.

In the "Religion of Reason," the concept of Jewish nationality takes its place in the scheme as an indispensable if subordinate category in mutual implication with the concept of Judaism as religion (Cohen, 1929: 417-429; 1972: 359-368). The treatment occurs in the chapter on "The Law" (*"Das Gesetz"*). The law dealt with in this section of Cohen's exposition is principally the "law of religion" (*das Gesetz der Religion*) (Cohen, 1929: 395; 1972: 340). This religion can also be referred to as the *Kultus* (Cohen, 1929: 417) which the English translation, in ways partially illuminating and partially obscuring, calls "Jewish worship" (Cohen, 1972: 359). Initially Cohen has in view Ezekiel's claims for a reconstructed sacrificial cultus, claims linked with Ezekiel's focus on national identity.

This biblical element, Cohen asserts, is transformed by classic Rabbinism which insists on the action of interior repentance; in the Rabbinic view, the sacrificial cultus was but an external symbolic representation of such repentance. Moreover, Cohen notes, an emphasis on repentance is central in the nineteenth-century Reform movement's quite proper renovation of "Jewish worship." Such worship centers on the cycle of festivals, culminating in the Day of Atonement as an occasion for repentance.

But, Cohen insists (1929: 417; 1972: 359), nineteenth-century Reform, unduly impressed by the standards of the modern civilized nations (*Kulturnationen*), characteristically has depreciated elements of Judaism that classic Rabbinism retained: those elements that are distinctive of the Jewish national character (*national juedische Charakter*). Advocates of Reform quite correctly judged that classically the law of the cultus is associated with national identity as well as repentance. Advocates of Reform quite correctly saw that this implied the isolation of the Jews from the surrounding environment. Where early and mid-nineteenth century advocates of Reform went wrong, Cohen insists, was in recommending the complete dissolution of the national element in Judaism. That recommendation subverts their desire to preserve Judaic worship (*Gottesdienst*). The religious element can be preserved only in conjunction with Jewish "nationality," the "ethnic" element in present-day parlance.

This ethnic element, the people Israel, is significant not alone for the preservation of Judaic worship. The people also has a mission, a task to perform among the nations. The people is the bearer of the universally valid ideas of prophetic ethical monotheism: the one God, his universal moral will requiring respect for all persons, and the social goal of a messianic humanity, mankind united under the standards of justice. Classically and in the present period of anti-Semitism, this mission encounters opposition and the people suffers. But the people must persist in its mission. Indeed, precisely in the German culture of the World War I period, Cohen contends, Judaic monotheism must contest the claims of Christian monotheism to be the only monotheism, the "absolute religion," to use Hegel's terms. This Judaic contesting of Christian claims protests against assigning absolute status to any cultural form. Jews contend for a cultural pluralism in the nation (Cohen, 1929: 423; 1972: 364).

Thus Judaic ethical monotheism is, in the modern sense, religion attentive to individual piety, but also attentive to communal religiousness, to the relation of worship and ethnic identity, and to the religious-cultural mission of the Jewish people.

I propose now to indicate why in the strictest conceptual sense Cohen's ethical monotheism is prophetic ethical monotheism. I have indicated already in treating the derivation of a religion of reason from the biblical sources that the prophetic stage of Israelite religion is, according to Cohen, religiously unsurpassable. The prophetic writings are the normative center for organizing the biblical religious literature. But Cohen also insists that in the conceptual sphere the prophetic faith and ethos provide beliefs and religious-ethical principles which, according to Cohen, are directly available to modern man and still pertinent. These key beliefs are a belief in a universal history and the belief in messianic humanity as a social goal.

According to the biblical prophets, there is a universal history, contingent upon and under the judgment of the universal moral will of God. This monotheistic conception of a universal human history, differentiates prophetic belief from the polytheistic world of religious myth. Myths, Cohen stipulates, retail stories of the beginnings of individuals and of worlds and stories of the final other-worldly destiny of individuals. The world of myth lacks a sense of human solidarity and a concern for this-worldly life. Prophetic monotheism, in a sharp break with the world of myth, focuses on a universal, this-worldly history. Israel's God requires mankind to conduct social life according to standards of universal justice which properly govern the whole of humanity.

According to the prophetic ethos, economic and social impoverishment of man is mankind's besetting ill and the major deviation from the divine will. Mythological polytheism is preoccupied with death and the fateful guilt of the individual; prophetic monotheism asserts human solidarity and decries man's impoverishment. The prophetic cry for justice demands rectification of the situation of impoverishment.

The prophetic social goal for humanity is a messianic humanity, a just human society expressing human solidarity. The prophetic literature envisages an individual messianic figure in a messianic epoch. Proper idealization permits excision of the messianic figure. (Liturgical reform in the Reform movement had already done that.) The goal of messianic humanity is an ideal goal of social justice toward which human ethical and social action is eternally directed. It is a this-worldly goal which will never be realized, only approximated. As an ideal goal, the notion of messianic humanity judges every particular realization of social relations. Nonetheless, programmatically, Cohen recommends a revisionary Marxist form of socialism as the contemporary application of the prophetic principles of social justice and approximation of the goal of messianic humanity.

These elements of prophetic belief and ethos, especially the ideality of the notion of messianic humanity as a social goal, have a bearing on the idea of God in Cohen's scheme. I have previously noted how the idea of God functions as a postulate in a neo-Kantian postulatory scheme of ideas as hypotheses. I now suggest further that in Cohen's concept of God the mode of ideality prevails over the mode of actuality (to use terminology Cohen would probably not fully endorse). To refer to God's ideality is to refer to that feature of oughtness in the divine will as universal moral will. This predominance of oughtness in the idea of God correlates with the notion of the social goal of an ideal humanity, a goal that stands in critical relation to any historical actualization. There is a symmetricality between the ideal of messianic humanity and the predominance of the mode of ideality in God.

In my judgment, Cohen's idea of God and of the divine ideality are not the only concept of God appropriate to a Judaic ethical monotheism. In certain respects, Cohen's concept is idiosyncratic and not typical of other late nineteenth-century proposals for Judaic ethical monotheism. On the other hand, Cohen's scheme exhibits a remarkable internal consistency and, in my judgment, his neo-Kantian mode of modernizing Judaism is one of the perennial modern options for Judaic belief.

One final observation is in order about Cohen's ethical monotheism. It has not only religious concentration and intensity but also inclusive cultural import. Cohen is convinced that Judaic ethical monotheism, not Christianity, is the most appropriate religious basis for modern culture as a whole. As I shall show in Chapter IV of this monograph, Cohen is heavily preoccupied in his book on the "Concept of Religion" with the unity of cultural consciousness. The argument is cast principally in terms of the integration and cohesion of various diverse human powers and fields of cultural activity in the consciousness of a single unified self. Cohen also refers to the unity of diverse elements of culture in a totality. But he is hostile to all forms of cultural theory that find the unity of culture in some immanent totalizing principle. The idea of God is a critical principle that stands against all absolutizing of a finite totality. Cohen's is a critical monotheistic theory of society and culture.

In this sketch of Cohen's proposal for ethical monotheism, I have moved from his method of correlation and his employment of the idea of God in the total system of philosophy; to his derivation of a religion of reason from the sources of Judaism; to his claims about Judaic monotheistic religion, attentive to individual piety but social in its religiousness and oriented toward universal history and the social goal of messianic humanity.

I turn now to the first element of Ernst Troeltsch's proposal for a Christian radical monotheism, his attempt to locate a systematic point of departure, the "essence of Christianity," and to organize properly the theological system. These methodological and procedural considerations parallel Cohen's interests in the derivation of a religion of reason from the sources of Judaism and his employment of the method of correlation. I shall then turn to the principal elements of Troeltsch's radical monotheism, noting Troeltsch's distinctive version of the late nineteenth-century Protestant claim that Jesus' religious and ethical proclamation and that of the early Church refocuses and universalizes the prophetic belief and ethos.

Then I shall turn to Troeltsch's presentation of the Christian concept of God as transcendent moral will whose essence is love. This basic concept of God, as I shall indicate, is given a distinctive tenor by reappropriating elements of the Pauline-Augustinian teaching about God. Finally, I will note the surprising fact that the Troeltsch who proposes to modernize Christian belief by presenting a concept of God principally drawn from the Hebraic elements in the Christian sources is simultaneously powerfully attracted to the alternative neo-Platonist emanationist tradition in Christian theology.

Troeltsch works out his version of ethical monotheism in the latter phase of the middle period of his authorship, during the concluding days of his tenure as professor of theology at Heidelberg and during the very early days of his tenure as a professor in the Philosophical Faculty in Berlin. The documents from which I draw my account of Troeltsch's views are his classic essay in 1916 on "The Faith and Ethos of the Hebrew Prophets" (1925a); its companion piece on the faith and ethos of primitive Christianity and the Ancient Catholic Church, "Die alte Kirche" (1925b); and the *Glaubenslehre*, his systematic theological lectures at Heidelberg in 1911 and 1912 (1925c). Further, Troeltsch published in 1912 a revised version of his earlier essay "Was heisst 'Wesen des Christentums'?" (1922c), available now in English translation (1977). As Walter E. Wyman's recent *The Concept of "Glaubenslehre": Ernst Troeltsch and the Theological Heritage of Schleiermacher* (1983) shows, the "Essence of Christianity" essay bears directly on the systematic statement of the *Glaubenslehre*. My own presentation at this point is informed by Wyman's.

In stating his systematic point of departure, Troeltsch as a systematic thinker invokes the notion of the "Christian principle." Such a notion of "principle" implies both the recognition of the cumulative deposit of a developing tradition and a critical judgment about what is primary in the tradition and what is significant for the future. Troeltsch as a historian of the Christian ethos is impressed by the variety and plurality of Christian religion, Eastern, and Western, ancient, medieval, early modern, and modern. No single essence of Christianity can be extracted from the scriptural documents. Indeed, Troeltsch insists, with only slight exaggeration for effect, the essence of Christianity changes in each epoch. In primitive Christianity, one finds two major impulses: Jesus' radical eschatological preaching with its insistence on relating all finite realities to the transcendent will of God; and the Pauline focus on the cult-figure of the Christ, present to the community through baptism and eucharist. These initial impulses are reexpressed in various contexts as the Christian tradition encounters and appropriates diverse patterns of thought and life and enters into "compromises" with those patterns.

When Troeltsch moves from the work of the historian and reflection on the work of the historian to the work of a systematic thinker, he acknowledges that systematic thought requires selection among varieties of Christian belief. Such selection requires responsible risk-taking. In the *Glaubenslehre* he chooses to interpret Christianity as radical prophetic monotheism; yet he is constantly aware of an excluded possibility, the neo-Platonist emanationist scheme of Eastern and medieval Western theology. In fact, he finds in that scheme of creaturely egress from and regress to God some advantages in thinking through Christianity as a religion of redemption.

Troeltsch's selection of resources from the tradition is further shaped by his estimate of the modern sensibility. Modern man is not occupied with death and other-worldly immortality as is the man of the Ancient Church. Nor is modern man primarily concerned with that oppression by the religio-moral law and the resultant guilt that compels Luther to seek a gracious God. Modern man, living in a vastly expanded physical universe and with a sense of the aeons of geological time and a post-Darwinian awareness of the origin of man, is fundamentally doubtful about the significance of his very existence as a moral personality. A proper modern reinterpretation of Christianity will show that Christianity provides significance to man as moral personality by relating him to the one God. That is the point of departure for the interpretation of Christianity as a monotheistic religion of redemption. But there is an ambiguity in Troeltsch's view. When he treats this-worldly historical moral and religious life, both individual and social, his view of Christianity as a religion of redemption is strikingly similar to, if in crucial ways different from, Cohen's

Judaic ethical monotheism. When the discussion turns to the final eschato-
logical significance of moral personality, Troeltsch is attracted to the neo-
Platonic emanationist tradition of creaturely egress from and final regress to
God.

In Troeltsch's systematic work, nothing corresponds strictly to Cohen's
method of correlation which determines the whole system of philosophy. Nor
does Troeltsch, in the *Glaubenslehre*, exhibit a flair for theological archi-
tectonic comparable to that of Troeltsch's theological hero, Schleiermacher.
But Troeltsch in the *Glaubenslehre* does give sophisticated attention to the
proper organization of the theological system.

Troeltsch's presentation of the body of Christian belief in the
Glaubenslehre is, as Wyman has recently demonstrated (1983: especially 59-
71, 97-170), in the tradition of Schleiermacher. Like that of Schleiermacher,
Troeltsch's is a theology of consciousness. There is no Christian knowledge of
or participation in the divine essence, even in revelation. One speaks of
Christian "thoughts about God." Further, like Schleiermacher, Troeltsch is
concerned with the interconnection and coherence of the whole body of Christian belief. What status then is given to the concept of God, and how is this
concept related to other themes? The concept of God is the central preoccupation of the *Glaubenslehre*. That is, Troeltsch's *Glaubenslehre* is radically
theocentric. Here Troeltsch stands in contrast with his theological hero
Schleiermacher, who gives Christomorphic shape to the whole body of Christian teaching by presenting the central Christian religious affection as a consciousness of sin and grace, and then examining as well that feeling of
creatureliness ingredient as a presupposition in the Christian religious consciousness of sin and grace. Troeltsch's theology is not Christomorphic in
Schleiermacher's style. Nor, incidentally, is Troeltsch's theology Christocentric in the sense that Christological doctrine is the center of the system,
informing every other doctrine. Troeltsch's thought is radically theocentric, not
Christomorphic in Schleiermacher's style nor Christocentric in Barth's.

But there is nonetheless another unavoidable element in Troeltsch's
thought: the significance of the historicity of Jesus for the life of faith. Thus
one must inquire: What is the relation of Troeltsch's radical theocentricity and
the mediation of Jesus the Christ? Here the opening section of the
Glaubenslehre on "Jesus Christus als Gegenstand des Glaubens" is critical.
Jesus the Christ, according to Troeltsch, is that point in human history when
the monotheistic faith of Israel's prophets is brought to a singular religious
intensity and interiority, broken free from its ethnic matrix and made available
to mankind as a whole. Jesus as faithful man is the mediator of faith in the one
God to the whole of humanity. That is what Troeltsch signals by locating the
two coordinate chapters on the "Religious Meaning of Israelite Prophetism"
(1925c:97-99) and on the "Meaning of Jesus for Faith" (1925c:100-117) in the

preliminary sections of the *Glaubenslehre*.

Further aspects of the concept of God are elucidated successively in the sections on the Christian concept of God (1925c:127-239) and the Christian concept of the world (1925c:240-278). In the latter, Troeltsch insists on a fundamental distinction between God and the world. The system is completed with the presentation of the Christian concept of the soul (1925c:279-325) and the Christian concept of redemption (1925c:326-364), plus two concluding fragments on the Christian doctrine of religious community (1925c:365-377) and on "Fulfilment" (1925c:378-384).

I proceed now to an exposition of the principal elements in Troeltsch's version of ethical monotheism. Troeltsch presents a distinctive version of the late nineteenth-century Protestant claim that Jesus' religious and ethical proclamation and the proclamation of the early Church refocuses and universalizes the prophetic belief and ethos. In the essay on the "Faith and Ethos of the Hebrew Prophets" Troeltsch establishes an initial point crucial to the understanding of that claim. According to Troeltsch, a distinctive feature of Hebraic ethical monotheism is the component of an active and vital human moral activity responsive to the demands of the divine moral will. But Troeltsch disagrees with that conventional view, put forward by late nineteenth-century biblical critics, that holds that the prophets state principles for organizing a just society. The requirement for an active and vital activity, Troeltsch holds, clearly does differentiate the prophetic ethos from any monism that prescribes quietism. But the prophetic demand for responsive moral action is paired with an attitude of indifference, even hostility, to culture. Historically, Troeltsch asserts, that attitude is to be explained in terms of the prophets' attempts to apply to a new urban setting the simpler standards of semi-nomadic and agricultural society.

This claim about moral strenuousness paired with cultural indifference in the prophetic ethos bears directly on how Troeltsch describes the reappropriation and refocusing of the prophetic tradition in the preaching and moral instruction of Jesus. Troeltsch does not fundamentally deviate on this point from the stereotypical views of all late nineteenth-century liberal Protestant biblical critics and theologians. First-century Judaism is assumed to be dessicated, moribund, standardized, and principally concerned with external conformity to legalistic demands. Only Jesus revives the prophetic heritage in the first century. But working within that stereotype, Troeltsch has some novel and sophisticated things to say. First of all, he is, by 1916, ready to accept completely the revolution in interpretation of Jesus' proclamation effected by Johannes Weiss's radically futuristic eschatological interpretation of that proclamation. But the indifference to culture of Jesus' proclamation is not unrelated to the prophets' views properly understood; for the prophets too are culturally indifferent. Standing in the prophetic tradition, Jesus radically interiorizes and individualizes the prophetic demand, while breaking it free from ethnic particularity. Jesus demands total devotion (*Hingabe*) to the one God. That devotion is to be given priority over any orientation of the self in devotion to finite realities. Such total devotion to the one God is not in conflict with but rather compatible with energetic moral activity.

The implications of this interpretation can be worked out in two directions: one relating to the assertion that for Troeltsch the claim of Jesus is identical with the ethics of conscience, the other relating to Troeltsch's translation of the Christian notion of redemption into the thought-forms and problem-world of Kantian and Hegelian idealism.

H. Richard Niebuhr in *Christ and Culture* (1951:183) contends, without extensive elaboration, that for Troeltsch "the claim of Jesus was identified with the ethics of conscience." I take that to mean that Troeltsch holds that the very particular, historically conditioned proclamation of Jesus, conceptually alien to the modern world, nonetheless uncovers something constitutive of human selfhood: only in singular devotion to the one God is man properly oriented. Moreover, this orientation should inform all of the self's moral activity.

This line of argument is connected with Troeltsch's distinctive view of that redemption that Christian religion affords. As Wyman's recent interpretation of Troeltsch points out (1983:142), Troeltsch holds that man's highest purpose, attainable only through religion, is to achieve that authentic human freedom that entails a transition from finite-egoistic creatureliness to a self surrendered to the divine will. This transition means a bursting of the limits of the natural self and the self's transformation. The problem-world of this formulation is that of the Kantian analysis of the freedom of the moral self over against necessity in the realm of physical causality and that of the Hegelian vindication of spiritual selfhood and community in contrast to nature. Troeltsch adopts these Kantian and Hegelian themes but gives them a new turn, a turn informed by Troeltsch's interpretation of the proclamation of Jesus and his restatement of the Pauline-Augustinian theme of Christian conversion. The self's creaturely moral personality can only be sustained and properly oriented through radical devotion to God. Such devotion breaks open the normal self-enclosure of the self, effecting a conversion of the creature which is his redemption.

This stress on devotion to God and conversion of the creature prompts Brian Gerrish to assert that Troeltsch's system is dominated by the problem of human transcience and that Troeltsch's concept of redemption is disengaged from moral considerations (1976:118, 119). Gerrish is further convinced that Troeltsch's concept of redemption moves toward pantheism, not moral theism. I should not wish to deny the ambivalence in Troeltsch's view, but I am disposed to emphasize more strongly than Gerrish the strain in Troeltsch's thought which Gerrish calls the anti-pantheistic: the emphasis on man's "relative freedom to make the world's purpose which is the will of God, his own moral task" (1976:119). Troeltsch is a Christian, prophetic, radical monotheist.

I have thus far presented Troeltsch's distinctive version of the claim that Jesus' religious and ethical proclamation refocuses and universalizes the prophetic belief and ethos. In continuity with prophetic teaching, Jesus recommends singular devotion to the one God. He also normatively exemplifies such devotion. This singular devotion can also be interpreted in terms of redemption which achieves authentic freedom in transition from finite-egoistic creatureliness to a self centered on the divine will. These prophetic, Synoptic New Testament, and Pauline themes all stress man in relation to God and God construed from such a relational perspective.

I turn now to another way of viewing these issues, to the "concept of God" as presented in the major section on that subject in the *Glaubenslehre*. Here Troeltsch treats what traditional theology calls the divine essence and attributes. God is principally to be conceived as moral will whose essence is love. It is the conception of the divine essence as love that prevents the concept of the divine will from lapsing into arbitrariness. Moreover, only in the context of conjoining will and love can the divine holiness be properly construed (1925c:138-329).

Troeltsch presents a transcendent God, radically distinct from and other than the creaturely world. The world's existence is contingent on the divine will, and thus at the heart of the Christian notion of God there is a certain fundamental irrationality. But God's will is purposive in realizing the good. God envisages a world-plan that is being accomplished even though that plan is not discernible in detail to man. Man's appropriate response as moral being is to adopt as the orientation for his own moral will that realization of the good God is accomplishing in the world.

The vindication of the Christian concept of God as moral will proceeds in two ways: by displaying the Christian notion of divine will typologically in contrast to two other types of monotheism, Judaic and Islamic, which also construe God as transcendent moral will; and by showing, interior to the Christian thought-world, what it means to opt consistently for the voluntaristic, in contrast to the substantialist-rationalist, tradition in the Christian teaching about God.

Troeltsch implicitly assumes modern man will recognize the superiority of the Christian view of God, though at the time of the presentation of the *Glaubenslehre* lectures Troeltsch is moving away from the hard apologetic of his earlier years. At the outset he had claimed it to be demonstrable that by its inner dynamic the concept of God, expressed in such various ways in the religions of mankind, moved inevitably toward greater spiritualization and moralization and to greater differentiation of God from the world. At the time of the fashioning of the *Glaubenslehre*, Troeltsch comes to a less hard form of apologetic: modern Western man will surely recognize the pertinence of the Christian concept of God for the European culture-circle and for modern Western man (Wyman, 1983:135).

The Christian conception of God as moral will is to be preferred to two versions of the notion of God as will that Troeltsch qualifies as arbitrary: the Judaic-Rabbinic and the Islamic. Rabbinic Judaism, according to Troeltsch, takes over the prophetic conception of God; but, instead of breaking free from the prophetic association of the will of God with the destiny of a single ethnic group, Rabbinic Judaism confirms that defect. Troeltsch is disposed to press very hard on this asserted Judaic lack of universality, while confidently claiming the virtue of universality for Christian religion. The relentless critique of Judaism on these grounds is curiously at odds with Troeltsch's increasing insistence on the historical particularity and conditioned character of Christian religion.

Judaism's identification of God's will with the destiny of a particular ethnic group makes Judaism arbitrary. Judaism is also arbitrary, Troeltsch claims, because it is a statutory religion. The divine commandment is spelled out in highly specific ritual as well as moral laws. Here one sees the persistence of Mendelssohn's characterization of Judaism as "revealed legislation" and of Kant's taking over Mendelssohn's view in Kant's own designation of Judaism as statutory religion.

According to Troeltsch, the Christian conception of God corrects Judaic arbitrariness by insisting that the essence of God is love. Troeltsch claims that the New Testament testifies to a breakthrough of the divine love to humanity as a whole; this breakthrough of divine love establishes a permanent relation of covenant between God and humanity as a whole. Thus the loving will of God is universal in principle. That point being secured, Troeltsch concedes that each action of the divine love directed toward man is particular. That pushes Troeltsch to take seriously the logic of the Pauline-Augustinian doctrine of predestination.

The Christian concept of God as moral will is vindicated not only in contrast to Judaism but also in contrast to Islam, which in its own distinctive way is also arbitrary. In Islam, the divine will is interpreted as a will that determines human fate. The element of irrationality in the divine will is controlling. Islam details certain minimal religious duties but does not secure a fundamental connection between the divine will and human moral activity.

Typological contrast with Judaism and Islam thus establishes certain features of the Christian concept of God as moral will. Troeltsch also chooses to give a consistently voluntaristic cast to the doctrine of God when selecting among the elements of the Christian tradition. This voluntaristic cast is to be preferred to the rationalist-substantialist alternative within the tradition.

The notion of the divine will implies a moral requirement made by God on the self which demands a response from the self. Such a requirement does not compromise human freedom which, properly understood, is theonomous freedom. (Troeltsch uses this exact terminology.) That means the aligning of the human will with the divine will.

Beyond such general indications, Troeltsch has, in this context, little to say about the specific content of the divine requirement. As I shall show in Chapter III, a complete ethical theory combines, according to Troeltsch, an ethic of the conscience oriented toward devotion to the one God with an ethic of objective values. Western institutions display such values which have emerged in the West under the impact of the Christian ethos.

Thus the voluntarist, in contrast to substantialist-rationalist, cast of Troeltsch's doctrine of God is indicated by the prominence given to the divine requirement and the corresponding theonomous conscience. That voluntarist element is more extensively developed through Troeltsch's adoption of classic themes from the Pauline-Augustinian tradition. Troeltsch adopts the Pauline-Augustinian theme of the conversion of the self from a self-enclosed life "according to the flesh" to a life in the Spirit oriented toward God. Troeltsch of course moves to this theme from his Kantian view of moral freedom and his Hegelian understanding of the spirit in individual and communal forms. Conversion, he repeatedly insists, is a possibility univerally open to all humanity. Here Christianity differs from Judaism's ethnic particularity. But, in fact, Troeltsch observes, such conversion to God is actual in certain individuals and not in others. That compels him to pay attention to the logic of the Augustinian doctrine of faith, election, and predestination. Troeltsch is thus constrained to acknowledge a qualification of his account of the intention of God's moral will directed to humanity universally: the particularity of the electing God's election of particular selves in distinction from others.

Troeltsch's conception of God as moral will whose essence is love is linked to a distinctive conception of the divine holiness. Once again, Troeltsch displays the Christian view in a typological description which differentiates this view from other religious and philosophical views. In Christian religion, the good and absolute holiness coincide. The holy God is the archetype of the good. In contrast to the Stoic and Confucian views which see a moral order immanent in the cosmos, Christianity holds that the order is grounded in the divine will.

The Christian conception of the divine holiness also shapes the relation of faith and moral life within the world of Christian faith and ethos. Acknowledgment of the divine holiness keeps the Christian view from lapsing into moralism. Here we have no merely negative prohibiting commandment. The Christian responds to the demand of the holy and loving God who calls him to life. And lest it be supposed that one has to do only with strenuous demand, the message of forgiveness is at the center of the Christian consciousness. Indeed, the Christian consciousness passes quite beyond that adequation of offense and retribution by God characteristic of apocalyptic Judaism. Christian consciousness is not even at ease with the notion of divine reward for moral behavior. The holy and loving God is the forgiving God.

In rounding out the Christian concept of God put forward by Troeltsch in the *Glaubenslehre*, I turn to a final consideration: Troeltsch's attraction to the neo-Platonist scheme of the egress of the creatures of God and their final regress to Him. This is a scheme employed by Augustine and it is basic to Aquinas's theology. (Of course both thinkers insist that finite creatures, once brought into existence, live eternally before God.) In the modern world, as Brian Gerrish notes (1976), this scheme often receives a monistic pantheistic formulation.

I have already pointed to issues raised for Troeltsch by the presence in the Christian tradition of this neo-Platonist scheme of egress and regress of creaturely reality. In locating, as a point of departure, the "Christian principle," Troeltsch acknowledges variety in the Christian tradition and proceeds in the face of that variety. He opts for what he calls the Hebraic ethical monotheistic element in the tradition. But his attraction to the neo-Platonist option is so strong, I would now concede, that Troeltsch comes close to contradicting his initial ethical monotheist assertions. Thus his scheme is susceptible of being developed in a quite different direction. Troeltsch's dilemma here is the obverse of Schleiermacher's dilemma in vindicating Christianity as a teleological religion oriented toward moral action after Schleiermacher initially has opted for a notion of God-consciousness as a feeling of absolute dependence.

The egress-regress scheme is attractive to Troeltsch precisely in his effort to present Christianity as a religion of redemption, responsive to the problem-world of Kant's analysis of moral freedom and Hegel's delineation of spirit in self and community. The creature, Troeltsch asserts, is to be broken out of his self-enclosure and converted to an openness to God. This conversion reorients this-worldly life. But what of the destiny of the self? Troeltsch is extraordinarily tentative and experimental on this point. He expresses dramatically his sympathy for the Catholic notion of a continuing purgative life for the self after death. Indeed, he hails Dante as the greatest of Christian theologians in dealing with this issue. He even flirts with the notion of the transmigration of souls, a notion not entirely incompatible with the idealistic (Kantian and Hegelian) elements in his theory of man. Finally, I would judge, Troeltsch opts for a return of the self to its source, God.

Troeltsch, I have argued, presents Christianity as radical ethical monotheism. In this chapter I have concentrated principally on the moment of religious intensity in that radical monotheism and on the significance of the singular devotion of the self to God. However, Troeltsch's Christian ethical monotheism also reaches out toward an inclusive interest in culture and society. In this respect, there are parallels between Troeltsch's and Cohen's proposals for ethical monotheism. In Cohen's case, the universal cultural inclusiveness is related to his conviction that Judaism as a religion of reason is the most appropriate base for modern culture. Cohen works that out through a conception of the unity of the cultural consciousness of the individual self. He also indicates his antagonism to any theory of culture that finds the unity of culture in an immanent principle of totality granted the status of an absolute.

In Troeltsch's case, his radical monotheism cuts against identifying any particular culture with the divine will as the sole legitimate unitary Christian culture. In Troeltsch's judgment, each differentiated sphere of culture is to be permitted to stand in relative independence without the attempt being made to demonstrate that sphere's evident or implicit religious significance. That is what taking seriously the secularization of modern culture means. It is this feature of Troeltsch's thought that leads Hans Frei to speak of Troeltsch's "non-apologetic theory of culture" (1965). On the other hand, Troeltsch does elaborate a theory of society and culture closely tied to a Hegelian ethic of objective values made concrete in institutional structures. This theory is related to Troeltsch's view of how, on the basis of the affirmation of the Christian doctrine of creation, the Christian ethos comes to terms with and enters into compromises with various cultural and societal constellations.

Chapter II

THE PROPHETIC ETHOS
IN DISPUTE

Cohen and Troeltsch put forward major proposals for revising classic Western religious traditions. They recommend the reconstruction of their respective religious traditions of Judaism and Christianity as ethical monotheisms. In the case of each, that involves a fresh appropriation of the faith and ethos of the Hebrew prophets.

Moreover, each one has the work of the other in mind in setting out his proposals. A vivid and informative instance of Cohen and Troeltsch taking each other into account is documented in a dispute between them in 1916 and 1917 precisely over the proper interpretation of the faith and ethos of the Hebrew prophets.

In this dispute, the disagreements between the two thinkers are stated with a controversial sharpness that underscores the very significant differences between them, differences that are irresoluble despite major similarities in their proposals for ethical monotheism. In fact, the differences displayed in this dispute are so acute and are shaped in such a way that one is led to suspect one must probe for grounds of divergence extending beyond the two disparate interpretations of the prophetic ethos.

It is Troeltsch in his extensive essay "Glaube und Ethos der hebraeischen Propheten" (1925a) who provides the initial provocation for the dispute expounded in this chapter. Cohen replies in a brief but passionate rejoinder, "Der Prophetismus und die Soziologie" (1917a). Thus clearly the ostensible topic of the controversy is the proper interpretation of the prophetic faith and ethos.

The prophetic faith and ethos is not a minor item in the total perspective of either thinker. On the contrary, for Cohen the prophetic ideas of God, world history, and messianic humanity emerge in a religiously unsurpassable moment in the history of Israel's religion, and the prophetic writings are a decisively normative source from which the contemporarary thinker derives a religion of reason out of the sources of Judaism. For Troeltsch the central Christian authoritative norm, the proclamation by Jesus of the divine kingdom and the message of the early church recorded in the New Testament, must, for proper interpretation, be realigned with the prophetic faith and ethos of the Old Testament. This provides the point of departure for an ethical monotheism

29

which gives priority to the Hebraic element in the Christian theological tradition.

But the controversy is significant not alone for the reinforcement it brings to our grasp of Cohen's and Troeltsch's employment of the prophetic faith and ethos in their systematic proposals. It also furnishes stunning insights into convictions each thinker asserts with passionate fervor. Indeed, the controversy provides a clue to where some of Cohen's and Troeltsch's deepest differences lie.

Though ostensibly about the proper interpretation of the prophetic faith and ethos, the controversy also provides new evidence about each thinker's philosophical methods and his procedures for the interpretation of traditional religious resources.

Further, in inspecting the controversy in its entirety and in context rather than simply extracting from it certain doctrinal points, one discovers the immediate social and religious matrix in which each thinker is operating. One can see a thinker combating certain fellows within his own camp, as with Cohen's antagonism to Zionism. One can see each thinker struggling to formulate a theory of culture and society adequate to his religious commitments and to a proper construing of the political, social, and cultural situation.

The controversy began with Troeltsch taking an initiative. In 1916, he presented to the Berlin Society for the Study of Religion a lecture on the faith and ethos of the Hebrew prophets (Liebeschuetz, 1960:52). A protege of Cohen's, Benzion Kellermann, vigorously controverted Troeltsch's views on the spot. Troeltsch subsequently published his paper (Troeltsch, 1925a) in *Logos* (1916), a periodical devoted to the exposition of neo-Kantian views of philosophical and cultural issues. Troeltsch had been a cofounder of *Logos* in 1912 and was among its regular contributors. His publication of his lecture in this journal assured attention to the issue far beyond the narrow confines of technical biblical exegetes and Christian theologians. Cohen (1917a:481) attempted to place in the same journal an extended version of Kellermann's remarks. After some hesitation the editor finally refused the request and Kellermann published his essay as a pamphlet. Cohen was evidently passionately concerned to have his own say. He published his reply to Troeltsch, "Der Prophetismus und die Soziologie" (1917a), in the August 1917 issue of the distinguished new journal he was editing, *Neue Juedische Monatshefte*.

Though Troeltsch provided the initial provocation, I have chosen to present first Cohen's rejoinder to Troeltsch, "Der Prophetismus und die Soziologie." Such a strategy permits one to see Cohen selecting certain key items out of his portfolio of views on ethical monotheism. And one sees Cohen deploying these items not in the tranquillity of systematic exposition but in a situation where, quite uncharacteristicallly, he is openly distressed at finding his primordial certainties challenged.

In my exposition of Cohen's essay, I shall initially reconstruct Cohen's version of Troeltsch's argument and show how Cohen combats that argument. Cohen has sensitive antennae for the central issues in Troeltsch's essay. In many major respects, Cohen understands Troeltsch and knows precisely where and how Troeltsch's views threaten and challenge Cohen's own.

Cohen does not accurately represent the totality of Troeltsch's argument. But even the misunderstandings or omissions in his presentation of Troeltsch are instructive. They throw light on Cohen's fundamental commitments and point to basic disagreements between Cohen and Troeltsch; and they point ahead to issues treated in Chapter III in exploring grounds of disagreement between Cohen and Troeltsch despite their common interest in advocating ethical monotheism.

According to Cohen, Troeltsch interprets the prophets as expressing the ethos of a peasant society with a semi-nomadic past. This of course is not the society in which the prophets are presently situated, but the prophets appeal to this ethos and its standards of justice in order to articulate an antagonism against the city civilization of the post-Davidic monarchy and an antagonism against the great oriental despotisms currently threatening the life of Israel and Judah. Such an interpretation, Cohen contends, reduces prophetism to a mere by-product: a by-product of the social relations of that peasant society whose ethos the prophets appeal to and a by-product of those social relations of their own time which the prophets resent.Further, Cohen notes, Troeltsch combines his claim about the prophets' appeal to the standards of a simpler past with a claim about the relative indifference of the prophets to the current construction of a just society. Such a view of the prophets is, according to Cohen, a threat to a proper view of the prophetic ethos as a fundamental charter, a set of principles for a just, egalitarian society.

Further, Cohen asserts, Troeltsch's interpretation reads prophetic monotheism as no more than Israel's singular devotion to a tribal and national god. According to Cohen, everything is at stake in properly connecting the prophetic ethos with the prophetic breakthrough to a universal ethical monotheism. Troeltsch compromises the universal character of prophetic monotheism, calling into question its freedom from the narrow limits of tribe and nation. Troeltsch thus throws doubt on the validity of the prophetic breakthrough to ethical monotheism as an unsurpassable ethical and religious moment. The prophetic faith and ethos are thus radically relativized. By making the prophetic ethos the product of a particular set of social relations and by misconstruing the universality of prophetic ethical monotheism, Troeltsch challenges Cohen's conviction that the prophetic concepts of the one God and the prophetic principles of social justice provide a resource that can be appropriated by modern man as the principles for constructing a cosmospolitan, egalitarian, socialist, economically equitable modern German society.

Now, one might suppose that Cohen could deal with Troeltsch's challenge in a somewhat more subtle fashion, avoiding a direct confrontation. Cohen is after all becoming at this time very sophisticated about method in the derivation of a religion of reason out of the sources of Judaism. The Bible is not a philosophically systematic source. Religious truths are given literary expression in the Bible in ways distinctively suited to religion. Those truths must be brought to systematic statement. Such a process both permits and requires the contemporary philosopher to be quite open about what in the biblical source he finds valid according to the standards of universal moral reason and quite open about what aspects of ancient tradition must be excised if that tradition is to claim the attention of modern man.

But one must also note with special care that Cohen the philosopher is convinced that the modern autonomous moral consciousness can formulate a set of universally valid "timeless" moral propositions. Moreover, from the time of the first edition (1904) of the *Ethik des Reinen Willens* (Cohen, 1921), Cohen has assumed that at the core of the prophetic ethos one uncovers a comparable set of principles: principles of justice and respect for persons. Cohen will not permit these prophetic social principles to be relativized.

I turn now to a further consideration which helps to account for Cohen's fierce resistance to Troeltsch's interpretation of the prophetic ethos. Here one cannot rely on direct evidence from this short text of Cohen's. I point rather to a contention he put forward in his "Concept of Religion" (1915) just prior to publishing his polemic against Troeltsch; this contention Cohen also continued to develop in his lectures in 1917 and stated in published form in the *Religion of Reason*. Cohen contends that the prophetic ideas of God, world history, and messianic humanity are properly to be read in a cluster which also includes Deuteronomy and the distinctive concern of the Exilic prophet Ezekiel for individual piety, national identity, and the usefulness of the sacrificial system in structuring the repentance of the individual. Only by so clustering the biblical materials can they be properly shaped up for appropriation and idealization in a religion of reason. Troeltsch disrupts Cohen's sense of that grouping of materials which runs forward from the early writing prophets through Deuteronomy to Ezekiel. Troeltsch rudely shoves the writing prophets back toward their antecedents in earlier stages of Israel's religious life and social relations. That, I suspect, profoundly disturbs Cohen.

The full range of this disturbance can only be recognized if one recalls that for Cohen the Deuteronomic version of the Torah is the principal and normative giving of the law. Other earlier nineteenth-century Jewish proponents of Judaism as ethical monotheism had tacitly welcomed the view of modern Protestant university scholars (from DeWette onward) that the Pentateuch is a diverse and many-layered composition. These earlier Judaic thinkers quietly embraced the characterization of Deuteronomy as a distinctive composition connected in some fashion with the reform of Josiah in the seventh century before Christ (Sarna, 1975). But no Judaic Reformer or practitioner of the Science of Judaism embraced so boldly as Cohen the biblical critical estimate of Deuteronomy. For Cohen, Deuteronomy is not only the principal and normative giving of the law; it represents a deposit in Israel's public law of the principal motifs of the preexilic prophets. Deuteronomy read in this way is focused on obligation to the stranger, thus on sympathy with the totality of one's fellowmen, thus on love for all men who are creatures of the one God.

It is in fact the case that Troeltsch also in "Glaube und Ethos der hebraeischen Propheten" (1925a:59) links the impact of the prophets, the reform of of Josiah, and Deuteronomy. But Troeltsch cannot possibly have the investment of Cohen in specifying Deuteronomy as normative Pentateuchal Torah and a deposit of prophetic teaching. In fact, Troeltsch sees the activity of the Deuteronomic reformers like the teaching of the prophets as an attempt to impose, in a "utopian" fashion, simple clan brotherliness on an increasingly complex city civilization.

Moreover, in Cohen's judgment Troeltsch fails to appraise properly the prophetic notion of the remnant and to recognize Ezekiel's specific development of the notion of the remnant in the direction of a transformed national consciousness and renewed individual piety. Ezekiel moderates the earlier prophetic tendency to stress the norms of justice at the expense of ritual practice. Once the prophetic principles of justice have been established, sacrificial ritual, according to the teaching of Ezekiel, can be reaffirmed as useful in preserving the identity of the people and structuring its life as a "congregation." Further, within a reconstituted sacrifical cultus, the pious individual is envisaged as engaging in a life of repentance and self-purification before God.

This vision of the people so structured with its transformed national consciousness has shaped, according to Cohen, the mission of the people of Israel as the permanent and irreplaceable bearer of the perennially valid prophetic ideas of the one God and of one humanity with a single history moving toward a never completely realized messianic future, a fully just society integrated with nature. Troeltsch may note the remnant as a prophetic concept. But he fails to appreciate the distinctive conception of Ezekiel. And Troeltsch breaks the continuous link between the prophetic remnant and the enduring Jewish people.

Cohen's antagonism is intensified by Troeltsch's full-blown theory that prophetic tradition in its subsequent impact is diversified into three strains: Christianity, Islam, and Rabbinic Judaism. Cohen, not unfairly, further reads Troeltsch as holding that primitive Christianity is the normative repristination of the prophetic ethos. Although Troeltsch's view may not be a simple doctrine of the complete supersession of Judaism by Christianity, Cohen is deeply convinced that Troeltsch's view compromises the distinctive role of the people Israel as the permanently authorized carrier of the prophetic ideas of ethical monotheism.

Moreover, Cohen is specifically offended at Troeltsch's claim that the prophetic ethos can appropriately be seen to issue in the other-worldly ethos of primitive Christianity and in subsequent Christian other-worldly ascetic and monastic movements. Troeltsch's argument on this point is, as I have already indicated in Chapter I, very subtle and complex. According to Troeltsch in "Glaube und Ethos der hebraeischen Propheten," the prophets affirm God as that transcendent will who, in covenant and promise, requires corresponding activity on man's part and indeed requires that each specific individual response exhibit purity of moral and religious disposition. For Troeltsch, the principal features of the prophetic faith and ethos are the transcendence of the divine will, the goodness of the creation, relative indifference to the construction of culture, and resistance to the dominant cultural trends of the great empires and the political calculations of the powerbrokers. Later prophets are increasingly occupied with shaping an obedient remnant. That tendency, according to Troeltsch, comes to further expression in the radical eschatological proclamation of the kingdom of God by Jesus and in the attendant demand for appropriate dispositions in responding to that proclamation. Neither the classic prophetic nor the primitive Christian ethos, according to Troeltsch, is world-denying or mystical: neither focuses on a distinction between outer appearance and true inner reality. But, since in the prophetic ethos the whole of creaturely reality is contingent and dependent on the transcendent will of God, prophetic monotheism can issue in a radical monotheism with a certain other-worldly cast. And this radical monotheism comes later to be associated with modes of other-worldly "ascesis." Thus, according to Troeltsch, even Christian monasticism is not totally discordant with the prophetic ethos.

Such employment of the prophetic ethos as a justification for Christian other-worldly ascetiscism is, according to Cohen, historically unconvincing. What is more, it is an intolerable confusion that diverts attention from proper present appropriation of prophetic principles in this-worldly construction of a just and equitable society. At this point, Cohen acidly remarks, Troeltsch must be under the influence of the renegade Bergson and his sympathies for Christian mystics and other-worldliness.

There is another way in which Cohen's antagonism is intensified by Troeltsch's theory that the prophetic tradition in its subsequent impact is diversified into the three strains of Christianity, Islam, and Rabbinic Judaism. Prophetic monotheism, according to Troeltsch, came to expression in two major spheres of civilization: the Christian movement in its limited but inescapable impact on the world of Late Antiquity, followed by the Christian shaping of medieval and modern Europe; and also in Islamic civilization.

Troeltsch adds almost as addendum that prophetic monotheism is also preserved in Rabbinic Judaism. Each of the diverse continuations of the prophetic ethos—Christianity, Islam, and Rabbinic Judaism—has a certain legitimacy. But Troeltsch seems to find it most difficult to accredit Rabbinic Judaism as an authentic continuation of the prophetic ethos. Rabbinic Judaism, according to Troeltsch, insists on a continuing restriction of prophetic monotheism to its original base in the particular life of a national people, rather than permitting the prophetic principle gradually to dissociate itself from that base in becoming a universally valid account of humanity's fate in relation to the salvific will of God. Only by such dissociation, Troeltsch further implies, can the prophetic principle become a proper ingredient for an inclusive civilization. To all of this an anguished Cohen can only reply that it is another product of an "increasingly anti-Semitic epoch."

This implied disqualification of the Judaic version of prophetic monotheism as a base for civilization cuts directly against Cohen's own project of reinterpreting Judaism as a universal ethical monotheistic religion. Such an interpretation of Judaism as religion sees the Jewish people as instrumental bearers of ideas pertinent to the shaping of a total modern civilization: the idea of monotheism and the ideal of messianic humanity. If Troeltsch had properly grasped this, Cohen implies, he could not have come so close to disqualifying Rabbinic Judaism and its modern continuation as legitimate inheritors of the prophetic ethos.

Cohen sums all of this up in his complaint that Troeltsch's interpretation of the prophetic ethos reduces a universally valid doctrine of the one universal sovereign over man and nature to the particularities of the claims of a tribal god. Judaism as a religion is concerned with the relation of God and humanity and not simply with the exclusive relation between God and a particular people. The people Israel is a "servant of the eternal God as the servant of humanity as a whole." The Shema means the "Eternal our God is one. The one God is the God of all people. Our God is not our God, but, as the one God, he is the God of all men and all people" (1917a:399).

Although there is no direct reference to the matter in Cohen's text, I am convinced that Cohen has another objection to Troeltsch's "tribal" nationalistic reading of the Judaic tradition. Precisely at the time when Cohen is bringing to culmination the nineteenth-century tradition of interpreting Judaism as universal monotheistic religion with a merely instrumental role for the Jewish people, he is compelled to take up combat on another intra-Jewish front.

By 1916, Cohen is vigorously engaged in a fight against the Zionist recasting and reappropriating of the national element in the Jewish tradition. He is antagonistic to all forms of Zionism, whether Buber's Romantic cultural Zionism or Klatzkin's more straightforward political-national Zionism with its strong emphasis on Hebrew as a vehicle of national life. At the very same time he is in controversy with Troeltsch, Cohen is also disputing with Buber on the Zionist issue (Cohen:1916b; 1916c). Cohen is also under attack by his own philosophical protégé Klatzkin. Disenchanted with Cohen's wartime apologia on behalf of the spirit of German culture, Klatzkin deplores Cohen's contention that the spirit of German culture is a superior product of the philosophical scientific spirit of Plato and the prophetic ethos, by way of Reformation Christendom. Klatzkin is scornful of Cohen's advice that Jews presently must take a new and decisive step in shaping this cultural situation, pushing to fulfillment the culture's commendable tendencies by providing in Judaic ethical monotheism a purer version of the prophetic ethos than sixteenth-century Reformation of nineteenth-century Ritschlian Protestantism could provide. This is folly, Klatzkin insists. It is time for Jewish Zionist disengagement from *Deutschtum* and for the establishment of a Jewish national state in Palestine.

Cohen, it would appear, senses that Troeltsch's reinterpretation of the prophetic ethos, if it were injected into the intra-Jewish Zionist debate, would give aid and comfort to his Zionist foes. That is another ground for repudiating Troeltsch's views.

To sum up, the picture of the prophetic ethos Cohen presents in "Der Prophetismus und die Soziologie" (1917a) has two major features: the prophetic ethos as the source of principles for a just society, and the unbreakable linkage of this prophetic ethos with universal prophetic monotheism as the unsurpassable moment in the Judaic religious consciousness. This prophetic ethical monotheism can and should be reappropriated for a modern reconstruction of Judaism as a religion; such a reading of Judaism as religion contrasts with interpreting Judaism primarily or in any major way as a "national" phenomenon. In this context, the Jewish people are instrumental bearers of the prophetic ideas of the one God and the goal of messianic humanity. This is the Jewish contribution to the construction of modern civilization.

These convictions are fundamentally challenged by what Cohen takes to be Troeltsch's sociological reduction. Troeltsch's reduction of the meaning of the prophetic faith and ethos to a function of a particular social situation radically relativizes the truth claim of the prophetic ideas. This reduction is especially dangerous when it contributes to the national, tribal reading of the Judaic tradition. Such a reading grossly distorts the universalistic stress ingredient in the prophetic faith and ethos and delivers to the modern mind a gravely erroneous picture of the prophetic religious and moral resources.

Troeltsch's essay "Glaube und Ethos der hebraeischen Propheten" (1925a) will now receive its due, an independent exposition. Troeltsch's argument does develop according to its own logic. And indeed an independent review of the essay brings to the fore some of Troeltsch's most distinctive basic positions, especially his conception of a "prophetic principle" and its fresh expression in classic Christian thought and in his own thought.

Methodologically, Troeltsch's operation in this essay shows his ties with the Southwest Baden (Heidelberg), in contrast to the Marburg (Cohen and Natorp), school of neo-Kantianism. (Troeltsch's indebtedness to Rickert is crucial here.) As Cohen accurately judges, what Troeltsch says in this essay about method and what he asserts about the current moral import of the prophetic ethos constitutes yet another in the series of controversial exchanges between the two schools of neo- Kantianism.

Troeltsch proposes to differentiate the method he employs in this essay from a general trend he finds profoundly attractive but ultimately wrongheaded: a "positivist-empiricist" trend. Locke, Hume, and Comte are founding fathers of this trend. Its classic and current exponents interpret religious life and ideas as function of material and social conditions. This procedure, though there is much to be learned from it, Troeltsch finally rejects as reductionist. But neither is Troeltsch satisfied with a contrasting tendency classically associated with Plato, Kant, and Hegel. Exponents of this trend assert the independence of the "idea," whether in the Kantian or Hegelian sense of "idea," and see the idea present in or unfolding itself in cultural life apart from any dominant determination by material and social conditions (Troeltsch, 1925a:34-38). In expounding this second tendency, Troeltsch clearly intends to criticize Marburg neo-Kantians like Cohen. Troeltsch insists that perceiving the structure of social relations and the location of a group in a network of political power relations is invaluable in uncovering the origin and appraising the character of the group's religious life and moral standards. But the religious-ethical factor in history also has a relative independence not reducible to a function of social and material conditions. For instance, a prophetic "principle" takes on its own independent life as it is expressed in later religio-ethico-social complexes in different and quite novel situations.

I would judge that in these formulations Troeltsch acknowledges the requirement of the neo-Kantian for judgments which are universally valid, but he modifies that requirement in the direction of Rickert's attention to a variety of concrete cultural values. This reformulation attempts to absorb the newly emerging relativist critique of the claim to universal validity. Such a position clearly differs from Cohen's Marburg version of neo-Kantianism.

Another point where Troeltsch in this essay is at odds with Marburg neo-Kantians, especially Cohen, is in the matter of coordinating the Kantian social ideal of a universal humanity with a revisionary Marxist social democratic program (Troeltsch 1925a:53). (Cohen's socialism is thoroughly treated in Willey, 1978; Luebbe, 1963; Mosse, 1970) Troeltsch is not entirely unsympathetic to the revisionist Marxist critique of the abuses of social power in late industrial capitalism. Rather, in this essay, Troeltsch declares it naive to suppose that a Kantian reappropriation of the prophetic ethos provides a charter for socialism or for democracy for that matter. And Troeltsch does go out of his way to make that point.

But Troeltsch is at odds with Cohen's reading of the prophetic ethos not solely in terms of polemic against a certain kind of neo-Kantian method or with repect to proposals for directly appropriating prophetic principles for present socialist reconstruction of society. Troeltsch presents a version of the prophetic ethos itself fundamentally different from that of Cohen's. Troeltsch's distinctive interpretation centers on the "utopian" character of the ethos (1925a: particularly 58-60, but also 45-57) and the prophetic movement's relative "cultural indifference" (1925a:60-64).

Troeltsch's characterization of the prophetic ethos as "utopian" has proven both provocative and informative. Max Weber immediately endorsed Troeltsch's formulation of the issue in his classic study of *Ancient Judaism* (1952:455). Troeltsch's thesis was thus launched into the world of the general social scientific descriptive analysis of the great world religions, though it is usually to Weber and not to Troeltsch that the thesis is attributed. Within the professional guild of Old Testament exegetes, Troeltsch's thesis has provoked continued discussion. Troeltsch and Weber, it is acknowledged, have set a significant agenda for technical exegetes (Gottwald, 1964:355-358; the review of the technical literature here is especially intelligent and thorough).

"Prophetic politics," according to Troeltsch, is "utopian." Neither the pre-exilic prophets nor the prophets of the exile, to say nothing of the postexilic prophets, attempt to put forward a "social ethic." There is no appeal to a "law of reason" that, when applied, will shape construction of an egalitarian and socially just society. Rather, appeals are made to the ethic of brotherliness and neighborliness characteristic originally of a semi-nomadic past and instantiated to some extent in a simple agricultural society. Such appeals are intended to jolt individuals in Israel out of a complacent settling down in the patterns of Canaanite city life which are becoming normative for the post-Davidic monarchies.

The prophets also project a future free of war and conflict in which man in history is integrated with nature and all nations flow to Jerusalem to acknowledge the God of Israel as the one God of the nations. Beyond this, the projection of the future is quite lacking in detail. Moreover, it is not principally this projection of the future Troeltsch has in view in characterizing prophetic politics as "utopian."

The principal emphasis is, rather, on a critical principle: the prophets' relative "cultural indifference." All natural and social existence is, according to the prophets, radically contingent and under the sovereignty of the transcendent divine will. This does not imply a metaphysical dualism which depreciates the significance of this world and its political and social life. The whole creation is good. But the critical principle of relative "cultural indifference" authorizes a stance contrary to the dynamisms of Canaanite urban life and counter to the trends and values of the great oriental despotisms which ravage and conquer the two kingdoms.

An early case of such prophetic politics is first Isaiah's advice to the king. In this advice, the holy war tradition is transformed. A transcendent orientation toward the divine will is substituted for a this-worldly preoccupation with the clash of forces. The calculation of relative power relations is forbidden. That older holy war tradition which sees Israel's God as the real victor in every successful military clash is transformed into a call for reliance upon an act of God coupled with a call for a renewed and obedient disposition. Here Isaiah exemplifies the universal tendency of prophetic politics: opposition to taking cues from political necessity or from the allegedly inevitable working out of the dynamisms of great power cultural development.

Within this context, questions of theodicy arise. The prophets provide a theodicy with a particularistic cast. They do not speak in general terms about the reality of moral and metaphysical evils as a challenge to claims about the divine will supreme in power and goodness. Rather the prophets focus on the fate of Israel and God's vindication of His people in the face of the hostility or indifference of the nations. Structuring the problem of theodicy in this way, Troeltsch clearly implies, is a grave intrinsic limitation on the prophetic faith and ethos.

This observation about the particularistic cast of prophetic theodicy is linked by Troeltsch to a number of observations about Rabbinic Judaism as a continuer and bearer of the prophetic ethos. Rabbinic Judaism as an inheritor of the prophetic ethos exhibits a particularistic preoccupation. Troeltsch spells this out in the main text of the "Glaube und Ethos" essay and in an extended note, appended by the editor of the critical edition of that essay, on the "working out of Hebraism in Western civilization" (1925:320). Two forms of the continued historical expression of prophetism, Troeltsch insists, can be properly called encapsulation. One such form is the "apocalyptic" with its rigid and predetermined timetable for divine action; the other the "talmudic" encapsulation which occurs, according to Troeltsch, when a pariah-people at the margin of a larger civilization develops an in-group ethic.

The introduction of the in-group and pariah-people conceptuality prompts a further consideration. If Troeltsch contends that even at its point of origin the prophetic ethos is an appeal to the brotherly norms of simple clan society in the face of urban complexity and hostile great power sophistication, is he endorsing Nietzsche's view of the genesis of Jewish and Christian morals in *ressentiment?* Troeltsch is very much aware of that possible reading of his interpretation, and he is at pains to deny that the origin of the prophetic faith and ethos can be reduced to the sentiment of *ressentiment*. But he does claim that after the period of the "second great catastrophe"—the destruction of the

Temple, the removal to Yavneh, the final failure of the Bar Kokhba rebellion—the Jews can be designated a "pariah-people." Troeltsch specifically invokes Max Weber's "sociological category" developed in his "Die Wirtschaftethik der Weltreligionen" (*Gesammelte Antsaetze sur Religionsoziologie*, Bd. III [1921], p. 288) (Troeltsch, 1925a:41). (See Weber's classic elaboration of this view in Weber, 1952:336-355, 417-420.) According to Troeltsch, in the life of a people existing on the margin *ressentiment* does come to play a role in the elaboration of an in-group morality (1925a:39-42, 62). Troeltsch even invokes in this connection Sombart's thesis about the distinctive role of societally marginal Jews in the origin of the capitalist ethos in the West (1925a:62), though he does not make the slightest serious attempt to adjudicate the complex issues of evidence and interpretation.

From Philo to Mendelssohn, Troeltsch goes on to observe, there have been attempts by this "ghetto-Judaism" to break through into Western culture but the inhibitions have always been powerful. Rabbinic Judaism insists on clinging to a Jewish national entity as the matrix for sustaining monotheistic faith. That tendency flawed the original prophetic faith and ethos; it continues to flaw the ethics of classic Rabbinic Judaism. Moreover, Troeltsch remarks, this national element is currently taking on renewed independent life in the "living problem of Zionism" (1925a:62). Troeltsch does not seem disposed to make nor, very possibly, is he well enough informed to be able to make subtle differentiations among the forms of Zionist ideology.

If he judges the central tradition of Rabbinic Judaism to be a flawed form of the prophetic faith and ethos persisting into the modern epoch, his attention and sympathy are nonetheless powerfully drawn to other forms of what he calls the continued efficacy of "Hebraism" in the Occident (1925a:820, 821).

At the beginning of the modern period in seventeenth-century Europe, Troeltsch claims, it becomes evident that "Hebraism," despite and in addition to its traditional mixture with other elements in the culture of Christendom, has a newly emerging independent role to play in modern culture. In fact, at this point a "principle of radical monotheism" most clearly emerges. Troeltsch has in view Jewish thinkers marginal to the Rabbinic community, especially Spinoza's "monotheism and his disinterested love of God." But Troeltsch is especially alert to a new role for the Old Testament. The Hebrew scriptures, traditionally transmitted in the West as the church's book, can now have a new impact in the shaping of Western culture. This impact is quite apart from attachment to any religious community, Christian or Judaic. Troeltscch alludes specifically to the "newly rediscovered nature-poetry of the Psalms" and to Herder's *Spirit of Hebrew Poetry*. And near the end of the honor roll of fresh appearances of the spirit of Hebraism, Troeltsch places Kant's ethos. To this, I would judge, Cohen would give the most emphatic assent, though Kant himself might initially have been a little startled by the asserted affiliation.

Moreover, Troeltsch, I would judge, sees his own constructive theological project as evidence of "the continued efficacy of Hebraism in the Occident." Or as he puts it in this essay: for the Christian "idea-world" to be credible to men of the present this "idea-world" must be stripped of its "gnostic, supra-natural and mystical-sacramental elements" (1925a:521). What is required is a theism that sustains man in his personhood: a Christian "Hebraism."

The working out of that larger project I have already investigated in detail in Chapter I. Here I complete the exposition on its own terms of Troeltsch's essay on the prophets in order to document fully the items in controversy with Cohen.

Troeltsch in this essay refers to a "prophetic principle," detached from the original matrix of prophetic writings and also disengaged from involvement with the fate and destiny of the particular people Israel. He provides a sketch of how that detachment occurred and its bearing on the development of the Christian theological tradition.

Recall that for Troeltsch the prophetic faith and ethos interconnects the divine rule, relative cultural indifference, and an increasing focus on obedient disposition in response to the divine demand. This is the prophetic faith and ethos which is transformed and renewed in the preaching of Jesus and the primitive Christian community. This preaching of Jesus and the primitive Christian movement, set as it is in the framework of radical eschatological expectation of the imminent inbreaking of the rule of God, gives to the prophetic ethos a universal extension and a final intensity. The prophetic ethos is broken free from ethnic limitation; and the requirement of purity of individual disposition is stated with unprecedented rigor.

According to Troeltsch, the full logic of the Christian transformation of the prophetic ethos is only worked out in Augustine's theodicy, his doctrine of sin, and his reading of the history of universal humanity. To put it in terms of Troeltsch's interpretive principles, in the teaching of Augustine we see an example of a "law of cultural life": Augustine is able totally to "dissolve the ideal content of the faith of the Hebrew prophets from its original sociological life-form." In Augustine's teaching, the prophetic conception of God as transcendent divine will is retained, but sin is no longer specified as the apostasy of the people Israel from the covenant will of God. Rather in the process of its dissolution from its Jewish matrix, the prophetic doctrine of God has been linked with a "general doctrine of universal humanity's fate in bondage to sin." And the drama of humanity's fate is replayed deep in the interior conscience and consciousness of the individual. (The most recent Augustinian scholarship, I would judge, has only reinforced Troeltsch's reading of Augustine. Recent elaboration of this thesis stresses the decisive importance of Augustine's reinterpretation of Paul. Paul's interest in how the Gentiles also can be part of the people of God is transformed by Augustine into a psychological drama of everyman. Man in his efforts at self-justification is encountered by the divine grace.)

In his essay on the prophets, Troeltsch provides indications about his own way of reclaiming and redisplaying the prophetic principle—a way that differs from that of Augustine. The classic Augustinian appropriation of the prophetic principle focuses on the divine will and specific relation of that will to human selves in the context of the general problem of theodicy. Troeltsch handles the matter in such a way as to stress the appropriation of the prophetic principle for a theory of society and culture. He insists that in the prophetic writings one finds no programmatic hostility to this-worldly life and institutions. The prophets affirm the goodness of creation. On the other hand, the prophets express a "relative cultural indifference"; no particular pattern of social and cultural life receives unqualified divine sanction. According to Troeltsch, this relative cultural indifference is taken over into the primitive Christian faith and ethos. Proclamation of the kingdom of the transcendent God, originally framed in eschatological terms, implies the requirement of singular devotion to the one God. In subsequent development of the Christian faith and ethos, the radical eschatological element is expressed in the religious ethos of ascetic monastic movements reinforced by neo-Platonizing world-views. (I refer on these points to Troeltsch's pairing of his essay on the faith and ethos of the prophets with an essay on the development of the Christian ethos: "Die alte Kirche" [Troeltsch, 1925b]. This essay was also published in the neo-Kantian journal *Logos* in 1916/1917.)

However, Troeltsch asserts, in the primitive Christian ethos as in the prophetic ethos the other-worldly tendencies are modified and corrected by affirming the goodness of the creation. This legitimates attention to this-worldly life; and it issues in what Troeltsch, in technical parlance, calls cultural "compromises." In the ancient period, an alliance is struck with Stoic ethics. This alliance issues in a theory of the two forms of natural law, absolute and relative. In this view, absolute natural law must, under the conditions of sin, be modified and expressed in the requirements of relative natural law. This culture-affirming element in the Christian faith and ethos also comes to the fore in the construction of medieval Christendom.

Troeltsch incorporates in his own scheme both the "relative indifference to culture" found in the prophetic ethos and the affirmation of the goodness of the creation found in the prophetic ethos. The element of singular devotion to the one God and "relative cultural indifference" is worked out by Troeltsch in the notion of radical monotheism as a critical principle. Such a critical principle disqualifies the ultimacy of any creaturely reality, whether social or cultural. For Troeltsch, this prophetic principle of relative cultural indifference gives leverage against the heritage of Christendom. In the late nineteenth-century situation, that means leverage in breaking apart the fusion of the sacral and the secular advocated by the exponents of the "Christian state." In principle it could even provide leverage against the pretensions of Troeltsch's own neo-Ritschlian program for shaping in his own epoch an ethos totally permeated with Christian values through the instrument of Christian personalities operating in the public sphere. The prophetic principle opens the way to the conceivability of a religiously pluralist, secular society, though it is not clear how far Troeltsch is prepared to move along that road.

But Troeltsch appropriates from the prophetic ethos not only the element of singular devotion to the one God and "relative cultural indifference" but also the theme of the goodness of creation and of this-worldly institutions. The latter element is worked out in the framing of a social ethic that draws on the neo-Hegelian notion of structured "objective" ethos in which values are deposited and instantiated (Kasch, 1963:240-242). Whether Troeltsch can envisage a situation in which the structured "objective" ethos is not dominated by Christian values one cannot say with assurance.

Chapter III

GROUNDS FOR DIVERGENCE:
NEO-KANTIAN AND NEO-HEGELIAN
ORIENTATIONS IN SOCIAL ETHICS

The dispute between Cohen and Troeltsch about the proper interpretation and the legitimate contemporary appropriation of the prophetic ethos was read by at least some of their contemporaries as another chapter in a continuing controversy between two schools of neo-Kantianism, the Marburg school (Cohen and Natorp) and the Heidelberg Southwest Baden school (Windelband, Rickert, Troeltsch). That is a shrewd reading, despite the fact that the ostensible topic of the controversy is the prophetic ethos. In laying out their differences, Cohen and Troeltsch clearly display commitments to two divergent schools of neo-Kantianism.

What is more, observing the interplay between philosophical commitments, and the divergent views about the proper interpretation and the legitimate contemporary appropriation of the prophetic ethos, moves one to the more inclusive surmise that such divergent philosophical commitments are at work shaping yet other aspects of Cohen's and Troeltsch's total intellectual programs.

This chapter focuses on Cohen's Marburg neo-Kantian orientation as it comes to expression in his social ethical theory. In a parallel way, I will look at Troeltsch's distinctive compound of a Southwest Baden neo-Kantian theory of the relation of history and values and a neo-Hegelian objective teleological ethic of value. This investigation will exhibit differences between Cohen and Troeltsch as they spell out the societal and cultural implications of their proposals for ethical monotheism.

Cohen sets out a regulative social ideal which endorses and projects toward the future the principal impulses of modern Enlightenment society. Because this regulative ideal is expressed as a norm which never has been nor conceivably will be actualized in a particular form of modern society, Cohen's contemporary opponents in the rival school of neo-Kantianism see his social ethic as yet another case of that empty and abstract formalism which, they allege, is the typical defect of Marburg neo-Kantianism. With that charge in view, I will indicate in this chapter some of the ways in which Cohen relates his regulative ideal to particular situations.

Strikingly enough, Cohen faces not only the charge of abstract formalism but also a quite contrary charge which comes from a number of diverse quarters. The charge is brought against Cohen by his disciple and critic, the Zionist Klatzkin. It is also put forward by those who, after the fact, denounce German academics like Cohen who espoused the "ideas of 1914," endorsing the German cause in World War I. The charge is also picked up by critics like Gershom Scholem who dispute the actuality and deny the validity of a "German-Jewish symbiosis." All these critics charge that Cohen claims a co-incidence between "Germanism" and "Judaism" which is in effect a total en-dorsement of the German societal structures and cultural tendencies of his own time. That is, Cohen is charged with uncritically declaring his ideal to be fully actualized in the German society of his own day. Thus, I propose to show in this chapter that in presenting the relation of "Germanism" and "Judaism" Cohen is making a highly selective presentation of certain aspects of the European cultural heritage and setting out a regulative paradigm of the relation between "Germanism" and "Judaism" coupled with a regulative ideal for the development of German society.

Paralleling this analysis of Cohen, the investigation of Troeltsch focuses on how Troeltsch employs resources peculiar to Southwest Baden, in contrast to Marburg neo-Kantianism. Further, at least in Troeltsch's version, this Southwest Baden neo-Kantianism has absorbed certain Hegelian themes and procedures. What is more, in working out his full social-ethical theory, Troeltsch also espouses a neo-Hegelian teleological ethic of value. To be more precise, in this exposition I will show how, on the one hand, Troeltsch uses neo-Kantian categories of a "formal ethic of conviction" to reexpress certain basic themes of the proclamation of Jesus and the Christian moral life; but, on the other hand, I will show how Troeltsch claims that the totality of a Christian ethic and social theory cannot be adequately expressed within the framework of a neo-Kantian formal ethic of conviction. The categories of a neo-Hegelian objective ethic of value are properly called into play to indicate how certain values, grounded in human physical conditions and needs or in psychological situations and drives, are shaped by the idea of the moral good within the structures and institutional forms of family, the state, the order of production and ownership, and works of art. The Christian doctrine of creation and the concomitant conviction that social institutions are essentially good created realities, require, in Troeltsch's view, a turn to a neo-Hegelian objective ethic of value.

Moreover, when Troeltsch makes the turn to this objective sphere of *Sittlichkeit*, he is concerned with the process through which, in the sphere of human history and in the course of historical development, social values have been deposited and structured in institutional forms. In the light of the fact that this depositing has occurred, Troeltsch insists, contemporary man is required to inspect past history for such values. This framing of this re-quirement shows the impact of neo-Hegelian styles of thinking on Troeltsch's thought. But the neo-Hegelianism is joined with a neo-Kantian element. Such values, drawn from the inspection of history in the sphere of *Sittlichkeit*, do properly make a claim to recognition as absolutely valid.

The examination in this chapter of Cohen as a neo-Kantian social theorist and the inspection of Troeltsch's use of neo-Kantian and neo-Hegelian resources will finally lead on to a concluding set of considerations. Is there a distinctive affinity between Kantian modes of philosophizing and Judaism which makes particularly appropriate Cohen's attempt to reexpress Judaism in exclusively Kantian terms? Is there some distinctive affinity between Christianity and Hegelianism which impels Troeltsch in the direction of a neo-Hegelian objective ethic of value? Does Troeltsch's affinity for Hegelianism and Cohen's repulsion of Hegelianism disclose something of broader significance about the resources for and styles of modernization of Judaism and Christianity? And does Troeltsch's affinity for and Cohen's repulsion of Hegelianism further disclose something about the distinctive character of a permanent antagonism between Judaism and Christianity in the modern world? These are the issues I propose to explore in this chapter.

I proceed now to a more detailed examination of the thought of Cohen as Marburg neo-Kantian social philosopher. In such an interpretation of Cohen, my framing of the issues owes much to two informants, Henning Guenther and Steven Schwarzschild. Guenther's *Philosophie des Fortschritts: Hermann Cohens Rechtfertigung der buergerlichen Gesellschaft* (1972) is striking evidence of the renewed currency of Hermann Cohen's thought among present-day German social philosophers. Guenther's study, highly original and in many respects sympathetic to Cohen, restates Cohen's proposals for the interpretation, justification, and redirection of that modern Enlightenment and post-Enlightenment society which has its base in modern industrial structures and technology. Steven Schwarzschild's extensive article "'Germanism' and 'Judaism'—Hermann Cohen's Normative Paradigm of the German-Jewish Symbiosis" (1979) deals, as does all of Schwarzschild's interpretation of Cohen, with the interconnections of Cohen the neo-Kantian philosopher, Cohen the Judaic thinker, and Cohen the social theorist.

Guenther's *Philosophie des Fortschritts: Hermann Cohens Rechtfertigung der buergerlichen Gesellschaft* (1972) proposes a distinctive way of construing Cohen. Cohen's whole intellectual enterprise is here interpreted as an essay in the social theory of modern society. His work in logic, epistemology, and moral philosophy and his recommendations for the modernization of Judaic religion are secondary and take on their significance in relation to the primary purpose of setting out a social theory of modern society.

In this reading of Cohen, Cohen is the interpreter of that modern rational society of associated individuals which contrasts so strikingly with premodern traditional communities. The free citizen and in this sense the "bourgeois" is the typical figure of this society, which sees itself as emancipated from the traditional constraints of the past. Indeed, it sees itself as a locus for the continuing emancipation of its members. Kant with his conception of man as a member of a universal kingdom of rational ends articulates one feature of that society which Cohen sometimes calls its cosmopolitan element. That element Cohen clearly prizes very highly.

However, there is another dimension of Cohen's appraisal of modern society. Guenther signals that dimension by beginning his exposition of Cohen's thought with a chapter on "Capitalism and Socialism." The modern world with its individualistic ethos, Cohen notes, has, ingredient within it, disintegrative tendencies. Indeed, one could even speak of a tendency toward anarchy. The individualism that is to be prized in some spheres of life is not adequate for securing social cohesion in modern industrial society. In Cohen's view, Marx correctly saw that the dynamisms of modern industrial society were driving toward a further stage of development. But such a further stage, Cohen insists, need not necessarily be reached through catastrophe. Cohen also differs from Marx in rejecting the notion that only a historical materialist conception of history can provide an interpretive theory for the redirection of society.

Strenuous efforts are required in developing the elements of social cohesion in society. Nostalgia for the premodern community is an empty sentiment. Not community but society as the totality of all human relations and social relationships is the modern mode of social organization, and the development from community to society is irreversible. The state is required to serve societal needs rather than regarding itself as a self-justifying supreme value. About these fundamental directions in neo-Kantian revisionary Marxist social ethic Cohen is quite clear.

With respect to the details of a restructuring of relations of production, Cohen seems content to be quite unspecific. On the other hand, he is very heavily occupied with marriage and the family as a unit that contributes in modern society as in premodern to the building of social solidarity. Here it would seem that Cohen's specific attentiveness to the moral values of the Judaic tradition contributes directly to the character and balance of his social theory.

Cohen's basic interest is in employing resources initially developed in bourgeois culture, especially its conceptions of science, religion, and art, to direct humanity to a new stage. And he is insistent that religion is among the resources that can be so employed. To put the matter in a slightly different way, the development of a new stage of society is taking place within a cultural-social sphere which can still be designated with some propriety as Christendom. As a Jewish intellectual, Cohen is marginal to the life of Christendom; he can in that situation discern both dangerous tendencies and positive resources within society which are not so clearly evident to all observers. In this connection, Guenther, from the vantage point of 1972, draws parallels between Cohen and a subsequent generation of Jewish intellectuals also located on the margins of society, specifically Walter Benjamin and Theodor Adorno. But in contrast to this next generation, Cohen is more ready to credit the efficacy of religious and ethical motivations. In fact, his entire body of writing can be read as providing an apologia for the continued significance and functional value of religion in modern society. Cohen quite concretely is ready to do business directly with liberal Protestant Christianity. Insofar as German liberal Protestantism is reconstructing Christianity as prophetic ethical monotheism, Cohen can envisage what one might call a convergence of Judaic and Christian traditions. Reconstructed, these converging traditions can provide a religious and ethical resource for redirecting society.

Specifically in its "socialist" dimension, prophetic ethical monotheism provides a resource for the cohesion of society. According to Cohen, there is in prophetic monotheism a cosmopolitan element appropriately reexpressed in the Kantian moral tradition; yet in isolation this element could be disintegrative. But prophetic ethical monotheism also has a "socialist" dimension that gives priority to sympathy with one's fellow human beings in their suffering. In prophetic monotheism, individual love for God and the "absolute individual's" self-sanctification before God find their place within the matrix of human sympathy and a will to alleviate human impoverishment.

Moreover, as Guenther boldly and accurately points out, the suffering of humanity in general is not Cohen's only preoccupation. As Guenther notes in connection with Cohen's interpretation of the Servant poem of Second Isaiah, the Jewish people has, through its suffering according to Cohen, a "Christological role" to play in modern society. Guenther is, I take it, somewhat at a loss in knowing how to integrate this aspect of Cohen's thought with the broader motif of the social significance of sympathy. And I should judge myself that Cohen's thought on this point is not fully worked out.

Prophetic monotheism then engenders the affect of sympathy as a basis for social cohesion in modern society. Such prophetic monotheism corrects tendencies toward mere individualism in the Kantian tradition. Moreover, there are further ways in which prophetic monotheism complements the cosmopolitan humanitariansim of the Kantian tradition. Prophetic monotheism provides a strong focus on and direction toward the real historical future as the sphere of human activity and societal development. Prophetic monotheism provides a social goal, Messianic humanity, which is less individualistic in formulation than Enlightenment ideals. On the other hand, this goal is to be regarded, to employ Kantian conceptuality, as a regulative ideal.

In gathering up all of these various considerations, Guenther is especially instructive in showing how Cohen brings to bear on the modern situation one final aspect of the prophetic faith and ethos. Guenther has in view here a matter that initially appears to be narrowly and strictly religious in import: the prophetic critique of mythical worldviews. Mythical worldviews, in Cohen's interpretation of the matter, are focused on individuals and their fateful enmeshment in the sins of their fathers. The prophets effect a liberation and establish individual moral responsibility and direction toward the future. The prophetic worldview is deeply congruent with the deepest impulses of modern society as that society emancipates itself from the fateful grip of the past and constructs a situation in which human emancipation can continue. I turn now to further aspects of Cohen's construction of a neo-Kantian social ethic. Steven Schwarzschild's "'Germanism' and 'Judaism'—Hermann Cohen's Normative Paradigm of German-Jewish Symbiosis" (1979) frames several issues with particular vividness and boldness.

Cohen's neo-Kantian social theory postulates as a goal for humanity a regulative ideal never to be achieved but always approximated. The way Cohen employs such a regulative ideal is regarded by Cohen's critics as a crucial piece of evidence in a general indictment of Marburg neo-Kantianism. Marburg neo-Kantianism is charged with being excessively formalistic, abstract and empty. Marburg neo-Kantians allegedly give exclusive attention to the first formulation of the categorical moral imperative which requires the adoption only of those moral maxims that can also appropriately be generalized as a universal law of mankind. This abstract universality in ethics allegedly is exacerbated by the heavy preoccupation with logic and mathematics in Marburg neo-Kantianism. So runs that indictment which Troeltsch among others is disposed to press against the Marburg neo-Kantians.

There is another darker side of the matter which Schwarzschild's exposition of this issue points up. The allegation is sometimes put forward that this empty formalism is linked to the fact that the principal exponents of the Marburg neo-Kantian school, with the exception of Natorp, are Jews. Their formal abstract intellectuality is allegedly characteristic of the contemporary Jewish mind and its roots in the formal abstract intellectuality of the classic Rabbinic mentality. This exercise in folk-psychology is clearly open to a crude and dangerous anti-Semitic exploitation, and it was in some cases so exploited. On the other hand, there may be some small nugget of intellectually consequential truth in this slag. Indeed, Schwarzschild, as I shall subsequently show, uses the charge as a point of departure for some striking reflections on the fundamental compatibility of the Kantian tradition and Judaism as a religion of reason.

To return to the sphere of academic debate, this defect of abstract formalism, as Schwarzschild shows, is claimed to have consequences for such a matter as the technical historical scholarship of the Marburg neo-Kantians and consequences, more important, for their social theory. The consequence in the field of social theory is alleged to be the inability of the theory to make contact with and have an impact on social reality.

On each of these points, Schwarzschild makes some compelling observations. The abstract formalism of the Marburg neo-Kantians, the opponents claim, distorts the scholarly efforts of the school in their presentation of the history of philosophical thought. This abstract formalism also allegedly infects their handling of the data of religion. An *a priori* concept of what is to be found and who is to be favorably appraised among previous philosophical systems or in religious traditions skews the presentation of the historical evidence. Schwarzschild concedes that a highly sophisticated process of "idealization" is at work in these scholarly productions, but he is also insistent that this process is coupled with much hard philological and text-critical homework in the sources. (I have attempted to show the same thing in my discussion in Chapter I of the derivation of a religion of reason out of the sources of Judaism.)

The same abstract formalism allegedly informs the character and tone of the Marburg neo-Kantians' efforts to construct theories. In this connection, Schwarzschild adduces considerations of the sort presented here in Chapter I discussing the character of Cohen's system. The system may originate in logic and mathematics, but as the fulness of the mutual implication of concepts is displayed there is an ever more extensive effort to bring in concrete data. This is precisely the case with respect to the data of Judaic religious life and the classic Judaic religious texts. As Schwarzschild also clearly demonstrates, there is a parallel move when Cohen is developing his ethics and social theory. For those purposes, the crucial data is from the science of jurisprudence.

Thus, Schwarzschild is, in my judgment, quite right in insisting that this style of theorizing is not merely abstract and formalistic. There is an interplay between the "ideal" heuristic conceptuality and the data. Further, on the question of the alleged inability of the Marburg neo-Kantians to make contact with and have an impact on social reality, Schwarzschild chooses to read the record. The Marburg school, he insists, was the only school of neo-Kantianism that tried seriously to have a critical, reformatory impact on the redirection of society. The Marburg neo-Kantians were politically engaged. As Schwarzschild (1981:4) sums the matter up: "[Cohen's *Ethik*] formulates in considerable detail and systematically derives from its philosophic operations an ethically idealist program of socialism, non-Marxist or at least heavily neo-Marxist, which, though making a significant impact at the time and noted in the secondary literature, has been neglected to our loss, and, in any case, it has been historically tragically ineffectual. This socialism was launched into programmatic practice by Cohen himself and by his disciples in their non-academic endeavors. Eduard Bernstein, Karl Vorlaender, and the martyred Kurt Eisner were among the most notable fighters in this movement."

All these allegations about empty, abstract, critical, negative formalism come to a head in a major philosophical issue, an issue that can be stated in terms of the competing claims of the Kantian and the Hegelian mentality for the allegiance of the intellectual elites in the late nineteenth and early twentieth centuries. Once again Steven Schwarzschild states the general issue with clarity and cogency. Schwarzschild's formulation has special polemical sharpness because he makes two further assumptions: that only Marburg neo-Kantianism is commendably free of neo-Hegelian influences, and that the sort of Southwest Baden neo-Kantianism on which Troeltsch draws is deeply permeated by neo-Hegelian influences. Schwarzschild argues (1979:133):

> The most fundamental philosophical disagreement between Kantianism and Hegelianism concerns the nature of the "ideal" and "noumenon." For Kant these and connected notions are purely heuristic, regulative, normative, non-empirical, non-ontological. For his troubles he has been accused ever since of being "abstract," "unrealistic," transcendental in a pejorative sense, irrelevant by Hegel and all his followers, including the Marxists. They undertook to "bring the noumenon back into the world" as a so-called "concrete universal," as reason incarnate in "empirical," and above all as "the rational that is real (actual)."

Schwarzschild contends that Cohen resists all attempts to proclaim that the ideal has been actualized, whether in the Prussian state, the Germanic *Volk*, the Christian church as Hegel's "spiritual community," or in any other historical empirical entities.

With precisely this philosophical issue in view, it is startling and instructive to consider Cohen's most controversial effort to bring his social theory into contact with reality. The controversy swirls around Cohen's wartime efforts to provide a rationale for the German cause in World War I and to contend for a positive correlation between *Deutschtum* and *Judentum*. Cohen initially states his views in a 1914 essay on the "individuality of the German spirit" and continues his efforts in 1916 with a pamphlet on "Germanism and Judaism."

These efforts have opened Cohen and his fellow academics, including Weber and Troeltsch, to the charge that they simply endorse the German cause without qualification. In expounding the "ideas of 1914," they attack the "ideas of 1789," the French revolutionary ideals which they denounce as abstract and spiritless concepts of liberty, equality, and fraternity. Their advocacy of a distinctively German idea of spiritual freedom gives license, it is argued, to the expansionist, militaristic, economic, and political ambitions of Wilhelmine Germany. Subsequent critics of the "ideas of 1914" claim that the exponents of those ideas demonstrate the total bankruptcy of an intellectual tradition, a tradition that failed the crucial test of intellectual integrity and independence under the pressure of wartime patriotic hysteria.

In Cohen's particular case this issue becomes vastly more complicated.

Cohen is attacked by Gershom Scholem and other subsequent critics of the attempt at a German-Jewish symbiosis from quite another angle. Cohen is alleged to have fatally compromised the independence and integrity of the Judaic tradition by attempting to reinterpret it as a religion of reason suitable as a base for modern European society. This misguided project of Cohen's contributed, it is claimed, to the Jews' failure to assess accurately the peril they faced in that German environment which at last confronted Jews with such massive and deadly hostility.

In the context of these charges, Schwarzschild's contentions are especially provocative. He argues (once again in Schwarzschild, 1979) that Cohen is attempting to present a "normative paradigm" for a "German-Jewish symbiosis." That, Schwarzschild contends, is not to be confused with a blanket endorsement of all the tendencies of Wilhelmine German culture. Nor is it to be confused with a complacent attitude toward the situation of the Jews.

Schwarzschild makes much of the social location of Cohen as it contrasts with the social location of German Protestant intellectuals who also spoke up on behalf of the "ideas of 1914." Although both Cohen and German Protestant intellectuals were middle class, Protestant intellectuals had every reason to be complacently satisfied with their situation. In contrast, middle-class German Jews like Cohen were still in the process of *embourgeoisement*. They were in a social location marginal to society and they were objects of increasing anti-Semitic hostility. This situation provided them with a sense of critical distance and a reason for identifying their own cause with the cause of other excluded or exploited social groups.

Cohen never intends to nor does he in fact ever endorse every tendency in contemporary German culture and social life. He is especially critical of tendencies to celebrate a "will to power." Nietzsche is a particularly reprehensible and deplorable instance of such a tendency. Cohen believes it is possible to make a critical selection among the elements of German culture, stressing especially the humanistic tradition of Goethe and rooting the whole modern trend back in the heritage of Luther interpreted as a hero of conscience and the advocate of "internalizing" the ideal. This selective appropriation is to be controlled and critically shaped by Kantian philosophical principles.

It is at this point that Cohen adduces his own version of that most distinctive doctrine of nineteenth-century Western Diaspora Judaism, the "mission of the Jewish people." According to Cohen, the mission of the Jewish people in the Diaspora requires a positive effort to reinforce the humanistic, cosmopolitan tendencies of German culture by contributing to that culture the prophetic ideals of the unity of mankind and messianic humanity. Cohen expects that there will always be tension between the regulative ideal and any empirical actualization. That is why Cohen's proposal may be fairly called a "normative paradigm" for "German-Jewish symbiosis."

Given this reading of Cohen, even the reality of the Holocaust does not totally invalidate the principles on which his proposal rests. In my judgment, only a flat and unqualified decision that Jewish existence in the Diaspora has no rationale could totally invalidate those principles.

These then are the main lines of Schwarzschild's vindication of Cohen in the face of two quite divergent charges: that Cohen's position is an empty formalism and that it in fact lapses into an uncritical endorsement of late nineteenth-century German culture and a naive estimate of the situation of the Jews in the modern world.

I turn now to an exposition of certain aspects of Troeltsch's work as a Christian social philosopher and ethicist, presenting Troeltsch's work in such a way as to make evident the contrast between his proposals and Cohen's work construed as interpretation of modern society and as a projection of a normative paradigm for that society and the role of Jews and Judaism within it. Such an exposition of Troeltsch will by no means disclose a Troeltsch at odds with Cohen on every issue, but it will disclose a thinker who proposes to modernize Christian religion and affirm the modern secular world without totally abandoning the heritage of Christendom.

In Troeltsch's work, one finds a compound of neo-Kantian and neo-Hegelian themes and procedures. Troeltsch is far less interested than Cohen in producing a coherent philosophical system. Rather, the clue to Troeltsch's work is to be found in the interrelation between interpretation of the Christian ethos and reconstruction of a contemporary pattern of Christian belief and theory of the moral life. Such tasks require the adducing of neo-Kantian and neo-Hegelian themes and procedures.

Early in his career, Troeltsch indicates his independence in selecting among the philosophical resources he will use in expressing the Christian ethic in a modern idiom. In Troeltsch's judgment, even at this early stage, the principal options available for his purposes are the Kantian and Hegelian conceptualities. Within the neo-Rischlian movement with which Troeltsch was initially identified, it was generally assumed that Kant's ethic was the major philosophical partner in a reconstruction of the Christian theory of the moral life. But Troeltsch, in an essay in 1902 on "Grundprobleme der Ethik" (1922a), faults the Ritschlian theologian Wilhelm Herrmann for reducing the Christian ethic to an individualistic "formal ethic of conviction." Some aspects of Jesus' proclamation of the Kingdom of God and the concomitant ethical demand can, Troeltsch asserts, be reformulated in Kantian terms. Such Kantian resources can be used to state Jesus' radical demand for purity of intention and devotion to the one God. Or to speak the language of neo-Kantian value theory, the free personality is immediately and transhistorically related to ideal values. But it is a falsification to reduce the notion of the Kingdom of God to a purely individualistic concept centered in the interior life of the self. A social dimension is ingredient in the notion of the coming of the divine kingdom. Here Troeltsch invokes the prophetic dimension of prophetic Christian religion and insists that the kingdom implies a common goal for mankind. But Troeltsch does not develop further this social dimension of the Christian ethic directly out of the notion of the divine kingdom. Rather he moves to the Christian doctrine of creation and the affirmation that social institutions are essentially good as created realities. In working out the implications of these theological convictions, Troeltsch looks to what Hegel calls the realm of *Sittlichkeit* in contrast to *Moralitaet*.

As Troeltsch puts the matter, there are certain values that have their ground in human physical conditions and needs or in psychological situations and drives. In the course of the development of social life within the historical sphere in the Christian West, these drives have been shaped in a particular way, under the impact of the idea of the moral good, within the structures and institutional forms of family, the state, the order of production and ownership, and works of art. The values accumulated in these structures make a formal claim of obligation on the self. However, it is also the case that these are values that have been crystallized in temporally conditioned patterns. These values objectively deposited in social structures must thus be reinterpreted and redeployed in a way appropriate to modern life. But, to look at the matter from the other side, this structuring of objective values in past epochs of Christendom constitutes a commendable deposit of social values. In any new cultural synthesis in a secularized world, these values can and should, Troeltsch argues, play a role.

These fundamental positions espoused by Troeltsch in his 1902 essay on the "basic problems of ethics" continue to dominate Troeltsch's thought. His final work, *Christian Thought: Its History and Applications* [1923] speaks once more of the complexity of the Christian ethical consciousness which must appropriately combine the "morality of the personality and the conscience" with the "ethics of cultural values" (1957a:67-122).

To put the matter in terms that point up the contrast between Troeltsch's position and Cohen's, Troeltsch has recourse to a neo-Hegelian objective ethic of value in order to deal with the cultural values which have in fact been crystallized in various structures of Western Christendom. By contrast, a Judaic intellectual like Cohen does not have that sort of investment in Christendom and its heritage. Indeed, Cohen is wary of the oppressive weight of Christendom and its deposit of actualized Christian values.

In reexpressing the Christian ethos in a modern idiom, Troeltsch has recourse then to neo-Kantian and neo-Hegelian themes and procedures. But closer scrutiny of a methodological issue is in order. Troeltsch makes a methodological commitment, especially in the period from 1902 to 1915, which aligns him with the Southwest Baden, in contrast to the Marburg, school of neo-Kantianism.

According to the Southwest Baden school, the Marburg school does not fully credit the significance of the historical, in contrast to the natural, sciences. Windelband, a dominant figure in the Southwest Baden school, focuses attention on the historical sciences' picture-making ("ideographic") operation in presenting historical individuality. This ideographic operation contrasts with the "nomothetic" interest of the natural sciences in describing general uniformities and regularities in the cosmos. Building on Windelband, Rickert claims that the historically individual item is also the initial locus of value. Rickert does not hold, however, that standards of value simply emerge out of the total field of historically individual items. He wishes to assert suprahistorical timelessly valid values. The judging mind has an independent grasp of such values. According to Rickert, the project of the philosophy of history, as a special science of the principles of the historical universe and the meaning of this universe, is to correlate the capacity for judgments of value which transcend time with the multiplicity and fulness of history (Drescher, 1976:15; Beck, 1967:472; Anchor, 1967:192-194).

Troeltsch takes over into his own position this double concern for historically individual items as the initial locus of value, on the one hand, and for judgments of value that transcend time, on the other. As the English translation of Drescher's article on "Ernst Troeltsch's Intellectual Development" expresses it, citing page 24 of the German version of Troeltsch's *The Absoluteness of Christianity and the History of Religions:* "It is for this reason that history knows no values and norms which coincide with factual gerneralities, but knows these [values and norms] always only as generally valid ideas, as ideas claiming validity, which always appear in individual form and proclaim their general validity only in the struggle against mere factuality" (Drescher, 1976:16).

For Rickert, these norms of validity are regulative. Rickert is thoroughly neo-Kantian here. Troeltsch proposes to move a step further. The historical idea "demands a metaphysical resolution." The normative and generally valid cannot be defined simply as ideal norms; there must be reference to a suprasensible reality which "strains forward in concert with the spiritual kernel of the world." Thus Troeltsch proposes to link, especially in the period between 1902 and 1915, methodological and ontological commitments.

With these basic methodological commitments in view, one may profitably turn once again to Troeltsch's interpretation of the biblical and Christian faith and ethos. For precisely in such reinterpretation the commitments are exhibited. Take, for instance, Troeltsch's treatment of the prophetic faith and ethos. Troeltsch locates that faith and ethos in its original historically relative social situation. He goes on to argue for the emergence of a "prophetic principle," freed from its original historical context. This valid "prophetic principle" is to be seen as reexpressed in successive cultural constellations.

In the case of the Christian ethos Troeltsch points to successive historically relative cultural crystallizations of original Christian values in the structures and institutions of Christendom, and recommends that these received structures be inspected once again for values that can be brought over into a new cultural synthesis.

Thus this inquiry into Troelsch's method in interpreting the Christian ethos discloses a Troeltsch deeply committed to the position of Rickert and the Southwest Baden, in contrast to the Marburg, neo-Kantian school of neo-Kantianism. Such adherence to Southwest Baden neo-Kantianism does indeed move Troeltsch at a number of points in his writings to a negative appraisal of the "empty formalism" of the Marburg school; in the thought of the Marburg neo-Kantians, Troeltsch insists, the theory of knowledge is too exclusively determined by procedures drawn from logic, mathematics and the natural sciences, in contrast to the historical sciences. Granted this generally negative appraisal by Troeltsch of Marburg neo-Kantianism, it is especially intriguing to note what Troeltsch actually has to say in his one extensive review of a book of Cohen's, the 1916 work *Der Begriff der Religion im System der Philosophie* (Troeltsch, 1918).

In this review, Troeltsch does not relent in his determination to point up the distinctively Marburg neo-Kantian features of Cohen's work. But there is also, I would judge, a surprising and attractive disposition on Troeltsch's part to commend Cohen's work as a very significant essay in Judaic religious thought and to indicate, wherever possible, convergences between Cohen's work and Troeltsch's own. Cohen's project, according to Troeltsch, is to co-ordinate the systematic elements of the thought of the Marburg school with Judaic *Glaubenslehre*. (I believe the evocation of Troeltsch's hero Schleier-macher is deliberate.) The goal is to give expression to a "religion of reason" or an "absolute natural religion."

Cohen's attention, Troeltsch points out, is focused, in Marburg neo-Kantian style, on the "concept of religion." No attempt is made to build up a view of religion inductively on the basis of modern psychology or the history of religion. Cohen's interest is in the concept of religion within the totality of a rational philosophical system in which man's powers of thinking, willing, and feeling are critically examined with an eye to grounding their operation in rational necessities of thought. Cohen does not grant religion a totally inde-pendent status as the expression of a fourth distinctive human power. Cohen's commitment is to the treatment of religion in connection with ethics. But re-ligion provides a distinctive dimension to the operation of the human powers even if one does not grant religion an absolutely independent status. Cohen's whole program is worked out with primary consideration to the building up of a coherent culture in its totality rather than isolating religion as a mystical phenomenon or treating religion in "semi-medieval" Romantic fashion.

Troeltsch's presentation of Cohen's project is subtle and balanced. In the course of his evaluation, Troeltsch indicates his interest in making common cause with Cohen against late nineteenth-century interpretations of the character and significance of religion promoted by Schopenhauer and neo-Romantic enthusiasts for mysticism East and West. Such interpretations lack precisely the moral and culture-constructing interest Troeltsch and Cohen share.

What is more, Troeltsch does not, in this review, press the usual Southwest Baden charge against Marburg neo-Kantians, the allegation that an abstract *a priori* conceptuality totally controls and distorts Marburg neo-Kantian employment of the data of history. In fact, Troeltsch commends Cohen's increasing immersion in the data of Judaic religion and the attempt to bring that data to bear in reconstruction of contemporary Judaic religious life. Such a program is, Troeltsch suggests, not unlike his own attempts to move back and forth between the historical data of Christian religion and the vindication of the truth claims of the Christian religious assertions.

I have focused on Cohen and Troeltsch as social philosophers and social ethicists and upon those differences and similarities between Cohen and Troeltsch that come to light when one construes Cohen as a proponent of Marburg neo-Kantianism and Troeltsch as a proponent of Southwest Baden neo-Kantianism who also has some neo-Hegelian affinities. Now to some final considerations precipitated by such inquiry: Is there a distinctive compatibility between Kantian modes of philosophizing and the Judaic religious tradition? Is there a Judaic as well as a Marburg neo-Kantian component in Cohen's antagonism to Troeltsch's neo-Hegelian philosophizing? Is there an affinity between neo-Hegelian patterns of thought and Troeltsch's commitments as a Christian social philosopher?

First, is there a special compatibility between the Judaic religious tradition and the Kantian philosophical conceptuality? In my judgment, the answer is affirmative at least to this extent. Cohen as a neo-Kantian social philosopher is strategically placed to bring to culmination one of the most profound tendencies and aspirations of nineteenth-century Judaism in its process of modernization: the aspiration to display the Judaic tradition, in its prophetic monotheistic form, as a social ethic. That means interpreting Judaic prophetic monotheism as the source of principles and regulative ideals for the whole of modern society. That means pressing to the extreme the universalistic tendency in Judaism. This strategy is at considerable remove from those nineteenth-century movements in Jewish life and thought that regard the total complex of Judaic law even in the modern world as primarily a means for affirming the distinctive identity of the Judaic ethnic-religious group. Such a strategy is at considerable remove from those movements at the end of the nineteenth-century that propose to focus once again, through the repristination of the category of Jewish nation, on the particularity of the Jewish ethnic group.

To state this in a slightly different way, there is a special affinity between the Judaic religious tradition and the Kantian philosophical conceptuality if and as that tradition is construed as being in itself a continuing resource for the emancipation of humanity. (Emancipation in this reading of the matter is not merely something that happened to the Jews in their early modern history.) Such an emancipatory interpretation of Judaism focuses especially on the theme of messianic humanity and the openness of the historical future. In such a scheme, the notion of messianic humanity functions as a regulative ideal never fully actualized.

Such an interpretation of the Judaic tradition is clearly at odds with the powerful late nineteenth-century Zionist critique which regards the whole project of the emancipation of European Jewry as a failure. Such an emancipatory interpretation of Judaism is also at odds with the turn to more existential styles of interpretation soon to become current in the early twentieth century, whether in the more existential-ontological style of Rosenzweig or the existential-expressionist style of Buber. Moreover, in our time it is routinely claimed that the Holocaust certifies the desperately flawed character of a project like Cohen's. But I should think that such a project could only be entirely disqualified as a legitimate option for modern Judaism if existence in the Diaspora itself were ruled totally unacceptable. Moreover, Steven Schwarzschild argues that such a Kantian conception of the regulative ideal of messianic humanity might even be critically pertinent to the Israeli project of normalizing Jewish life.

Such neo-Kantian conceptions of the Judaic resource for a universal modern social ethic are clearly at odds, as Schwarzschild argues, with neo-Hegelian celebrations of the actualization of the rational, whether in the German Protestant culture of the early nineteenth-century or in the "Christian state" of the late nineteenth-century in Germany. I would judge, then, that there is indeed a distinctive Judaic as well as a Marburg neo-Kantian component in Cohen's antagonism to all neo-Hegelian social philosophizing, including Troeltsch's. This much can be said at the level of a social ethic.

To refocus the issue in terms of religious themes, a neo-Kantian position like Cohen's is at odds with the Hegelian claim that the concrete universal is actualized in the incarnation of the Christ and in the secularized form of modern bourgeois Protestant society. With this consideration in view, one may reflect once again on the neo-Hegelian element in the work of Troeltsch as a Christian thinker.

Troeltsch's is not a Hegelian Christology of the concrete universal. As a

Christian prophetic radical monotheist, Troeltsch intends to reformulate Christology in terms of the Christ as that point in human history where Jesus Christ the faithful one inducts the whole of humanity into the prophetic faith of Israel. Troeltsch's Christology is a radical monotheistic Christology, and it is expressed by Troeltsch with the aid of a formal ethic of conviction.

But there are points where Troeltsch's position does have Hegelian filiations and where Troeltsch is thus at odds with Cohen's neo-Kantianism. In a fashion typical of all forms of Christian thinking known to me, Troeltsch constantly doubles back to the point of origin in the Christ of the Christian faith in the one God. And he further assigns, in the *Glaubenslehre*, a normative status to subsequent Christian history as a religious source. Thus Christian religion, in Troeltsch's version and quite certainly in any other conceivable version, is by no means so exclusively oriented toward the open historical future as is Cohen's Judaism focused on messianic humanity.

Further, when Troeltsch turns specifically to a social ethic and to those social goods and moral virtues to be fostered within the this-worldly social institutions which the Christian doctrine of creation affirms as good created realities, Troeltsch expresses these convictions through a neo-Hegelian ethic of objective values focused in that realm of *Sittlichkeit* where in history Christian values have been deposited and structured. From one perspective, this is a way of affirming the goodness of creation and providing a Christian social ethical account of societal reality. It is a counterpoise to the exclusive attention to God and the ethic of inner conviction that appear to be dominant in the original Christian ethos.

But there is another aspect of things that becomes especially clear when Troeltsch is compared to Cohen. Troeltsch, the late nineteenth-century Christian thinker, is committed to the achievements of Christendom and to taking over those achievements into any new cultural synthesis. This commitment to the values actualized in Christendom is in tension with the radical prophetic monotheistic conviction that the real and the rational are never fully actualized in any finite constellation. And indeed that monotheistic reservation shapes Troeltsch's statement of a neo-Hegelian social ethic. But however radically monotheistic Troeltsch's position may be, there are within it these neo-Hegelian elements. These neo-Hegelian elements in Troeltsch's social ethic are a source of the antagonism between Cohen's Judaic universalistic conception of a social ethic and Troeltsch's proposals for a Christian social philosophy.

Chapter IV

ETHICAL MONOTHEISTIC THEORY
OF CULTURE AND SOCIETY

There is another aspect of the ethical monotheism of Cohen and Troeltsch: the inclusive interest in culture and society. Ethical monotheism as presented by Cohen and Troeltsch has, to be sure, a moment of religious concentration and intensity which stands in contrast to the inclusive interest in culture and society. Indeed, in Chapter I of this monograph, I have focused on monotheism as religion. This initial consideration of monotheism as religion establishes two points indispensable for understanding how religious concentration and intensity relate to inclusive interest in culture and society. First, ethical monotheism directs attention to God in contrast to every reality in the created world. Second, identifying and interpreting religion in a modern world in process of secularization involves, in the view of both Cohen and Troeltsch, reference to a distinctive aspect of the human spirit and to a discrete and clearly differentiated set of symbols, texts, and institutions.

That second consideration is uniquely modern. Classic Judaism insisted on the integral wholeness of Torah-directed life with no sharp differentation between religion and culture. But, according to Cohen, a properly modernized Judaism is best presented by referring to a distinctive dimension of human experience—not a fourth mode of *a priori* structuring of experience, independent of and in addition to the structuring at work in knowing, willing, and feeling, but at least a distinctive dimension of human experience. What is more, the distinctive dimension of human experience crystallized in Judaic religious symbols, texts, and institutions functions in a modern culture explicitly shaped principally by secular and Christian values.

Similarly, post-Constantinian Christianity was classically attached to the notion of a unitary culture of Christendom totally permeated by Christian belief and ethos. But Troeltsch acknowledges that a modern interpreter of Christianity in a world in process of secularization inevitably presents Christian religion as the expression of a distinctive power of the human spirit, crystallized in a discrete and clearly differentiated set of symbols, texts, and institutions.

Taking these features of the modern situation into account, it is arresting to find that Cohen's and Troeltsch's ethical monotheism nonetheless reaches out toward an inclusive interest in culture and society.

61

Thus, to state the fundamental issues of this chapter once more, with respect to religious concentration and intensity both Cohen and Troeltsch do insist on a sharp distinction between God and creaturely reality. Moreover, they both focus on a human self related to God, whether in a correlation of God and the "absolute individual" (Cohen) or a relation in faith between God and the individual self (Troeltsch). But this God-relation does not alienate the self from the world. Created reality, including human culture and society, is affirmed as good. Culture and society are the appropriate sphere of human activity. Indeed, monotheistic religion energizes the construction of culture. Thus, integral to Cohen's and Troeltsch's proposals for ethical monotheism is a culture-affirming and constructing impulse.

I propose then in this chapter to set out Cohen's and Troeltsch's theories of culture and of society and the state. How are these theories specifically mono-theistic theories? How is the theme of oneness played out? God is one. The human self achieves its integral unity in correlation with or in relation to God. The world is one integral whole and human history is, at least prospectively, the history of the whole humanity. Linked to all these claims is an attempt to sketch the unity of a totality of culture in the interrelation of its various elements. In the case of both Cohen and Troeltsch, such an attempt as this is a feature of their total intellectual programs.

A cautionary note is, however, in order. The full execution of the project of providing a theoretical account of the unity and interrelation of various elements in a totality of culture is by no means entirely accomplished. Moreover, I judge that the lack of full execution is not simply a matter of failure to follow through in performance on the announced project. Both Cohen and Troeltsch entertain a monotheistic reservation about providing too systematic an account of intraworldly reality. Admittedly in Cohen's case this may be less clear. Perhaps, as Rosenzweig and others have argued, Cohen is in danger of co-opting God into the totality of the system of ideas. Nonetheless I do read Cohen as entertaining a monotheistic reservation. Both Cohen and Troeltsch hold that no immanent system of totality can be permitted to rival God. Moreover, Cohen's and Troeltsch's awareness of a division between the religious and the secular in the modern world points to a distinctively modern instance of the irreducible plurality of the world. This a-wareness of irreducible plurality is a barrier in its own distinctive way against working out too tight a systematic account of an actual or prospective unity of culture.

But both thinkers do give an account of the unity of culture and the interrelation of various elements within it. And they do so in enough detail to make it profitable to look carefully at these accounts and to ask how and in what way these accounts are monotheistic theories of culture and society.

I turn now to Hermann Cohen's elaboration of an ethical monotheistic theory of culture and society and to his account of the unity and interrelatedness of various elements in the totality of culture. Implicitly such considerations as these are in mind throughout Cohen's entire philosophical authorship. Cohen slowly and carefully builds a System of Philosophy which includes an interpretation of each of the distinctive human powers: a logic of pure knowledge, an ethic of pure will, an esthetic of pure feeling. (The massive two-volume *Aesthetik* is completed in the second decade of the twentieth century, the same decade in which Cohen produces the writings on religion expounded in this monograph.) In this exposition, however, I will focus on Cohen's major book-length programmatic statement issued in 1915, *Der Begriff der Religion im System der Philosophie*. This book is usually adduced in sortng out, with an eye to discerning constancy of position or possible shifts, Cohen's various views on the relation of ethics and religion. I put forward here a different reading of the volume, a reading that does not attempt to do justice to all the richness and complexity of Cohen's analysis of the concept of religion but a reading that gives prominence to a neglected aspect of his argument.

In the "Concept of Religion," Cohen presents a theory of culture heavily occupied with the unity of culture. But instead of spelling this out in terms of the interrelations of institutions or even in terms of the interconnections of various cultural artifacts (or "objectifications," to use Hegelian terminology), Cohen focuses on consciousness, the "unity of cultural consciousness" and the interconnection of various human powers of cultural consciousness. This focus on the self's consciousness parallels Cohen's treatment of religion as a dimension within the experience of the self in its individuality, a dimension of experience that informs the whole range of experience.

Cohen's proposal is, to my knowledge, unique in the literature of nineteenth- and early twentieth-century Judaic religious thought and in the literature of early twentieth-century phenomenologies of culture. The nineteenth-century Judaic Hegelians might have found warrants for a comparable project, but they were principally occupied with demonstrating how Judaism, not Christianity, is the absolute religion for modern culture. Among early twentieth-century phenomenologies of culture, Cohen's project most clearly resembles Ernst Cassirer's *Philosophy of Symbolic Forms*, a phenomenology of culture developed in a tripartite scheme of a phenomenology of linguistic forms, an interpretation of mythical thought, and a phenomenology of knowledge. Indeed, in his own endeavor Cassirer is quite self-consciously Cohen's successor and legatee, and there are explicit acknowledgments of Cohen in *The Philosophy of Symbolic Forms*. But although Judaic ethical monotheism is, in my judgment, always implicitly on the horizon of Cassirer's work, Cassirer's essay is explicitly a descriptive neo-Kantian project without a religious agenda. Cohen distinctively combines the neo-Kantian powers with an explicit Judaic monotheistic theological interest.

Cohens' enterprise is no doubt, like Cassirer's, a neo-Kantian enterprise. Moving beyond what is taken to be a legacy of ontological dualism in Kant's own simultaneous affirmation of receptivity to the given and spontaneity of the self in ordering experience, Marburg neo-Kantians like Cohen insist on the productive role of the self in constructing a world, whether in the logic of origination with its matrix in the infinitesimal calculus, or in the autonomy of the self in giving the moral law to itself, or in artistic production as the supreme instance of human creativity.

But in addition to focusing on the self's powers, Cohen, in his theory of the unity of cultural consciousness, constantly brings to bear on the interpretation of the unity of the self's consciousness the idea of the one God. Indeed, correlation of the self with the idea of the one God is the ground of the self's awareness of the requirement of the never-ending task of achieving its own unity, including the unity of the self's cultural consciousness. Or, to adduce a theme constant in Cohens' work from the time of the *Ethik des reinen Willens*. God is the God of truth and as such he is the ground of the consciousness of the self's unity.

All of these claims may sound at first banal and common-place. But the claims take on controversial liveliness when one looks more closely at the German cultural situation in the late nineteenth and early twentieth centuries. The constrast between the views of Cohen and those of Max Weber on this issue is especially dramatic. Weber expresses a vivid sense of the conflict and ultimate incompatibility of cultural values in the modern world. Religious values, moral values, and esthetic values can no longer be perceived as coordinate and hierarchically ordered. Especially after Nietzsche's challenge, the idea of the beautiful and the idea of the good are now frequently perceived as antithetic. That which is beautiful and powerfully attractive is by no means always that which is morally good. Weber pointedly repudiates the heritage of Western monotheism and insists on describing the contemporary conflict and incompatibility of values as a reemergence of polytheism, a demythologized polytheism of plural value centers. It is in this general controversial context and in specific opposition to Nietzsche that Cohen reaffirms the task of achieving the unity of the self's cultural consciousness in correlation with the idea of the one God.

That does not mean that Cohen claims to read a self-evident coordination of the spheres of cultural values off the face of modern experience. Nor does he advocate a hierarchical ordering of cultural spheres and values comparable to the Thomistic schematic ordering of the social, the moral, and the supernatural-religious. There are tensions and polemical interconnections between various spheres. For Cohen, the center of cultural consciousness is the moral construed in a Kantian fashion. What is affirmed in the moral sphere has a critical impact in the esthetic sphere. And, while any separation of the religious and the moral is rejected and any independent assertion of supernatural religious values disavowed, the prophetic affirmation of the one unique God properly has polemical impact on the full range of cultural activity and value.

Moreover, the idea of the one God that Cohen brings to bear on the self's understanding of the unity of cultural consciousness is not simply the idea of God in his bare formal unity. Rather, in the development of the argument of the "Concept of Religion," the idea of the one God is progressively filled out more fully with the content of the Judaic religious tradition. That means a prophetic Judaic concept of God that is inextricably connected to the notion of an open future of humanity in this-worldly history and to the projected unity of Messianic humanity. It is this concept of God that properly correlates with an ethical consciousness which is also a social ethical consciousness focused on the redirection of modern society and the construction of a just rational emancipatory society.

In the full development of the argument of the "Concept of Religion," Cohen takes one particularly interesting final step in bringing into play not only the Judaic idea of God but also the Messiah-idea. In a treatment of the virtues, there is a move toward recommending what might be called the Messianic virtues. Such a recommendation implies a revision of that account of the virtues Cohen himself previously favored, an account structured around the Kantian notion of respect for persons. It is humility around which the Messianic virtues cluster. This shift of Cohen's toward the Messianic virtues is directly related to his criticism of the Nietzschian celebration of the will to power. Redemptive love suffering on behalf of another now comes into view as a possiblity for human moral action. This is the significance of the Judaic notion of the suffering of the pious. Such suffering pious are confident their suffering is not linked in a mythological fashion with a dark fate and an inherited guilt. They are confident that their suffering is not without significance for humanity and the future oneness of humanity.

Cohen spells this out further in his treatment of heroes, the heroes classically celebrated in literature and currently regarded as models. Modern men, and indeed Cohen himself in some of his moments, have a special affinity for Prometheus, that hero who exemplifies man's cultural daring and achievement and who suffers because he has challenged the gods. But Cohen brings to a climax his whole treatment of the unity of cultural consciousness in the "Concept of Religion" with a commendation not of Prometheus but rather of the servant figure of Second Isaiah as a hero and model. For Cohen, the people Israel in the modern world is the suffering servant who suffers in redemption of others. What in detail Cohen has in mind one cannot imagine—beyond his repeated insistence that Israel suffers hostility because of its devotion to the one God.

Cohen, I have thus far indicated, coordinates the unity of the self's cultural consciousness with the idea of the one God, and increasingly fills out the idea of the one God with the content of that prophetic Judaic concept of God inextricably linked to the open future of humanity in this-worldly history and to the projected unity of Messianic humanity. These claims bring Cohen into conflict with some dominant cultural trends of his own time. But there is another side to Cohen's case. With great delicacy and finesse, Cohen makes an apologetic case for Judaism, in contrast to Christianity, as the most adequate religious base for modern culture. One key aspect of that case for Judaism is that Judaism grasps more adequately the relation between esthetic and religious feeling and that Judaism protects more adequately than does Christianity both the integrity of the moral sphere and the otherness of God the Creator. Thus, in developing further this presentation of Cohen's theory of the unity of cultural consciousness, I turn now to Cohen's critique of Christianity as an inferior religious base for modern culture and to a more detailed examination of what Cohen has to say about the esthetic sphere.

In approaching Cohen's estimates of the relative religious superiority of Judaism over Christianity as a base for modern culture, it is necessary to recall that, with respect to institutional arrangements in society, Cohen is content to secure what he calls "tolerance" for a plurality of religious confessions. Moreover, he is much occupied with the dangers of a fanaticism that declares one's own religion the only true, the "absolute religion." But Cohen is willing to argue calmly and dispassionately that prophetic Judaic monotheism is the norm against which all religious claims, including all other monotheistic claims, must be tested. Judaism is normatively "pure" monotheism and as such constitutes a superior religious base for modern culture.

In Judaism, the concept of the one God is present in its "purity." The purity of the Judaic concept of the one God who is beyond all imagining stands in contrast to primitive Christianity's reintroduction of a mythological element in its doctrine of God becoming man. The prophetic protest against myth must be brought to bear against classic Christian doctrine.

Judaism's religious warrants for establishing the unity of mankind are also preferable to Christianity's. Judaism directly and without mediation correlates the unity of God and the unity of mankind. Christianity establishes the unity of mankind indirectly and mediately by linking the unity of mankind with the idea of Christ, mankind's unity thus being established only in and through Christ.

What is more, in its actual historical performance in the West, Christianity and its idea of Christ have introduced into human consciousness certain diremptions and imposed upon human consciousness severe conflicts. The linkage of the idea of the Christ with the mythological idea of original sin as fateful bondage has effected in the religious consciousness of the Christian believer so deep a fissure between man the sinner and man in grace that the believer must always struggle to maintain a sense of personal unity and cohesion. This distorting diremption is also present, Cohen insists, in the Hegelian restatement of the Christian theory of man.

Cohen's apologetic case in behalf of the superiority of Judaism as a base for culture and his critique of the inadequacies of Christianity is closely connected with his treatment of esthetic feeling. He is convinced that in the production of artistic creations, whether in visual art, literature or music, man is most vividly aware of his own capacity for "creativity," for "origination," for "production." Correctly understood and established in its limited but proper autonomy, such activity is unqualifiedly commendable. But the esthetic feeling involved in artistic creation has been perennially linked with a longing for the infinite and to a sense of man's boundlessness. Such a conjoining of esthetic and religious feeling violates the limits of man's proper creatureliness.

Such a mixture of religious and esthetic longing for the infinite is expressed in forms of mysticism which debilitate man's moral seriousness and cut the nerve of the impulse to the construction of culture. In the modern period, such a religious esthetic longing for the infinite has received an inner-worldly but nonetheless deadly restatement in Spinoza's pantheism. Such a conflation of religious and esthetic longing for the infinite is also expressed in a crypto-pantheistic form in Schleiermacher's *Speeches on Religion*, and the same basic error is repeated in the later Schleiermacher's proposal of a feeling of absolute dependence as the basis for a reconstruction of the Christian religious sensibility. Against other-worldly mysticism, mystical pantheism and Scheiermacher's reconstruction of the Christian religious sensibility as a feeling of absolute dependence, Cohen sets the classic prophetic Judaic monotheistic acknowledgement of man's finitude. Man and God are not ultimately identical. God and man are in correlation. God is other than man.

In the affective sphere then, the religious and the esthetic have been perennially conjoined and confused in inappropriate ways. At yet another point as well, the esthetic and the religious have been from time immemorial conflated in the mythical expression which is a fundamental element in religion. At the point of religion's historical origins and at many junctures in its development, human religiousness and the human imaginative capacity for mythical expression are closely linked. When Cohen refers to myth, he refers to stories about the coming to be of worlds and to stories about the fateful primordial fall of man. Myth is fundamentally backward looking, oriented toward the past. When myths speak of redemption, they speak of an otherworldly redemption of individual selves and lack a serious dimension of human solidarity in historical existence.

In his treatment of myth, Cohen's account of the cultural consciousness and its unity clearly differs from Cassirer's total inventory of the human powers including the power of mythical thinking. Cohen's account of religious mythmaking is always directly linked to the norms of prophetic monotheism. The activity and products of mythmaking in the religious realm are always presented as properly in the process of being shattered and surpassed in the interest of prophetic monotheistic purity. Further, this critique of religious mythmaking is frequently tied to a critique of classic Christological doctrine.

Thus Cohen's presentation of the prophetic critique of myth and his delineation of a proper view of the relation of the esthetic and the religious rounds out Cohen's account of the unity of cultural consciousness and the interrelation of elements within it; and the registering of these points establishes as well a key element in his case for the superiority of Judaism over Christianity as a base for modern culture.

In examining Cohen's case for Judaism's claim to be the proper base for modern culture, one further consideration is in order. Throughout this monograph, it has been reiterated that it is "Judaism" Cohen commends as a religious base for modern culture. But how is this "Judaism" expressed and made operative? As has been shown in some detail, when Cohen finally comes, in the last phase of his work, to think through a theory of the unity of modern culture in its totality, he talks in terms of human consciousness and of Judaic religion as a distinctive dimension of human experience informing the activities of knowing, willing, and feeling. For Cohen, whose historical horizon is bounded by Europe and who regards the Diaspora situation as normative for Jews in the modern period, it would scarcely be conceivable to advocate a culture and society in which Judaic religious beliefs directly form the charter for institutions of education and the state. For Cohen, it is individual selves, shaped by Judaic religion, operating in modern culture, who are the locus and bearers of those Judaic religious values and ideas that are properly to invigorate and shape modern culture.

I am proposing in this chapter to set out not only Cohen's theory of the unity of cultural consciousness but also his theory of society and the state and to establish as well the sense in which both these theories are monotheistic theories. Cohen's discussion of the unity of cultural consciousness is worked out in the "Concept of Religion," where he directly analyzes the unity of cultural consciousness in correlation with the idea of the one God. In this case, the task of demonstrating that Cohen's theory is a monotheistic theory of culture is thus quite straightforward and uncomplicated. In the case of a theory of society and the state, as distinct from a theory of culture, the matter of demonstrating that Cohen's theory is a monotheistic theory is less straightforward. Throughout his mature authorship Cohen makes a number of major theoretical points about society and the state. In examining some principal elements of what might be called Cohen's general theory of society and the state, an additional consideration will be kept in view: Are these elements of

Cohen's general theory of society and the state at least compatible with Cohens' mature views, expressed in 1915, about the unity of cultural consciousness and its correlation with the idea of the one God? I believe that at least compatibility is demonstrable. In fact, I agree with the view that, as Schwarzschild and others have recently argued, the general theory of society and the state contains itself tacit, and sometimes even explicitly acknowledged, monotheistic presuppositions.

In his theory of the state, Cohen presents as normative the conception of the state as a *Rechtsstaat* (Luebbe, 1963:104-106), a limited constitutional state in the tradition of eighteenth-century Enlightenment theory. Such a notion of *Rechtsstaat* is grounded in a prior acknowledgement of the "rights of man." This conception of the "rights of man" as prior to and not merely dependent on the state is correlated with the notion of *societas* as the most inclusive reality of social life. Moreover, within social life there are properly a plurality of centers of initiative, including the state. But the state is to be a limited state and Cohen is especially on guard against the pretensions, in theory and practice, of the *Machtstaat*.

In Cohen's scheme, the notion of *Rechtsstaat* functions as a regulative ideal even in a situation in which this ideal is not fully instantiated in the actual arrangement and functioning of institutions. The *Rechtsstaat* as regulative ideal stands in contrast to and in tension with the reality of the *Machtstaat* (Luebbe, 1963:105-111) and in opposition to the theoretical legitimation of the state as by definition normatively a *Machtstaat*. Cohen readily concedes that in late nineteenth-century German society there are still remnants of the medieval communal patterns of organizing life in various estates. Superimposed on these residues from the medieval and early modern past are the class divisions of modern industrial society. In important respects, the class controlling the means of production in fact also dominates in the state and employs the state as an instrument. But the regulative ideal of a *Rechtsstaat* can, Cohen believes, be increasingly institutionalized in a democratic state with a universal franchise in and through which the interests of all classes can be articulated. Cohen's theory envisages a perennial tension between the ideal of a *Rechtsstaat* as an egalitarian society and the various shifting forms of the *Machtstaat*. Cohen wants to redistribute social power and to deprive the state conceived normatively as a *Machtstaat* of its legitimating rationale.

The most fundamental notion in Cohen's social theory is that of "society," *societas*, or, if one is forced as it were by Toennies to choose, *Gesellschaft*, not *Gemeinschaft* (Schwarzschild, 1981:ix-xviii). Cohen conceives of *societas* as composed of a plurality of associations, of *Genossenschaften*, labor unions and cooperatives being the most commendable examples. The regulation of the interaction of such *Genossenschaften* is carried out in positive law and reflected upon in the science of jurisprudence. Positive law deals with legal persons or *persona*, in short with the general category of corporations, among the examples of which labor unions and cooperatives must be counted. Coordinate with the application to "corporations," positive law also deals with the individual man as "one equal member of the subclass of all its legitimate subjects, in his capacity as a *persona* and as a *homo*, i.e. as a ratio-legal, not as a physical entity" (Schwarzschild, 1981:x).

Through this conception of society, Cohen proposes to recognize a plurality of centers of initiative in society. But the ultimate regulative ideal of social life is a unified humanity. It is in this connection that another aspect of the theory of the state comes into play. Cohen insists that in the state and its unity the regulative ideal of unified humanity has a partial and provisional instantiation. This latter claim accounts for what is, in my judgment, the paradoxical character of Cohen's conception of the state. *Societas* is the primary catetgory for social theory. The state is properly a limited, constitutional state, a *Rechtsstaat*. But a very high status is assigned to the state and to its unity precisely because it is a provisional instantiation of a unified humanity.

Where, in all of this, is that category much in vogue in social theory in Cohen's own time, the category of *Volk?* As I see it, Cohen gives logical priority to the regulative ideal of a unified humanity, works back to the state as provisional and partial exemplification of this ideal, and only then comes to the concept of *Volk*. The *Volk*, according to Cohen, is the initial "socialization" of humanity, biologically based and first in the process of development. But normatively the state as provisional and partial instantiation of the ideal of unified humanity is a more primary reality and category than that of *Volk*. The state is not to be reduced to a mere organ of the *Volk*.

In line with this general theory of society and state, Cohen comes, from the period of 1870 onward, to give more explicit attention to an additional question: what social-theoretical interpretation of the Jewish people can he offer consistent with his overall views? In this regard, Cohen is increasingly open in acknowledging his desire to provide a rationale for the preservation of the distinctive identity of the Jewish people. And he wishes further to provide a counter to the charge that the Jewish people is an alien group defiling the purity and unity of the German *Volk*.

In working out this issue, Cohen insists that the Jewish people is indeed, to use the terminology of recent American sociology, a distinctive "ethnic group" and not merely a "religious confession." Cohen's own term, as I indicated in Chapter I, is *Nationalitaet*, not to be confused with *Nation* and the institutionalization of *Nation* as a state.

But the reality of the Jewish people cannot be reduced to one more instance of an ethnic group or *Nationalitaet*. For the presence of this distinctive ethnic group in society and culture has a special religious and moral significance.

The principal function of the Jewish people in their particularity is to be the bearer within the total society and culture of the ideas of monotheism and of messianic humanity as an ideal. These ideas and regulative ideals function, in Cohen's view, as permanent barriers against dangerous "totalizing" tendencies in culture and society. That is, these ideas and regulative ideals stand in critical judgment on all tendencies to ascribe absoluteness to a particular element within society or to ascribe absoluteness to the reality of the social process as a whole. Here then is a monotheistic protest against all totalitarian tendencies to idolatry.

In examining Cohen's general theory of society and the state, two further items claim attention: first, the relation between religious groups in general and society, especially as that relation may be expressed officially throught the state; second, a key juncture where general theory of society and state passes over into theory of culture and where once again the status of religious groups and their traditions is at issue.

In the matter of the relation between religious groups in general and society, Cohen, one would judge, clearly hopes for the emergence of a religiously "neutral" state and for a society that permits the operation of a plurality of religious groups with no civil disabilities for members of any group. In such a situation, no single religious institution would be formally linked to the state in a distinctive and exclusive way. Nor would any single religious tradition be seen to be the solely valid and indispensable religious element in culture.

If one turns to a key juncture where general theory of the society and state passes over into theory of culture, a further conceptual distinction comes into play. Cohen advocates a *Rechtsstaat* and he wishes to advocate a *Rechtsstaat* that is simply and without qualification a *Rechtsstaat* rather than a *Rechtsstaat* that is also a *Kulturstaat*. The conception of a *Rechtsstaat* that is also a *Kulturstaat* is current in circles with which Cohen has some ties of sympathy. This alternative view of a *Rechtsstaat* asserts that a *Rechtsstaat*, though a limited constitutional state, can and should also function as a *Kulturstaat*, a state promoting throughout society and culture, principally through educational means, uniform, agreed-upon values of the unitary *Volk*. This alternative view is put forward by political liberals. And among its major proponents are potential allies of Cohen on the religious front like the Liberal Protestant Troeltsch. Such conceptions of a *Kulturstaat* can, as they do in Troeltsch's case, even involve a recommendation for the institutional "separation of church and state." Thus these notions of a *Kulturstaat* can differ very significantly from the nineteenth-century notion of a "Christian state" where the warrants of political authority are derived directly from Christian belief, and a close institutional connection between church and state is insisted upon. But despite the differences between the notions of a "Christian state" and these liberal and

Liberal Protestant notions of a *Kulturstaat*, Cohen is still suspicious, I would judge, of this conception of a *Rechtsstaat* that is also a *Kulturstaat* promoting uniform, agreed-upon values of the unitary *Volk*. He may well suspect that the advocates of these notions have not abandoned the basic assumption that the German people is a Christian people, and an exclusively Christian people at that!

Cohen prefers rather to argue for a conception of the German people that can envisage the Jewish *Nationalitaet* as having a valid place within the total people. And he prefers to recommend a conception of the state in which the state as such has strictly limited distinctively political functions. Within that situation, the Jewish people through its ethnic and religious reality and individual Jews in their various roles convey to the culture the distinctive and universally significant ideas of ethical monotheism.

Troeltsch's ethical monotheism, like Cohen's, displays an inclusive interest in culture and society as well as religious concentration and intensity. In Troeltsch's thought as in Cohen's, despite singular concentration of ultimate devotion on the one God in contrast to all creaturely reality and despite a focus on the self in the establishing of the self's unity through that singular devotion, there is no culture-denying attitude. The created reality of cultural and social life is affirmed as good and culture and society are regarded as the appropriate spheres of human activity.

The characterization of Troeltsch's views on culture and society here presented features aspects of Troeltsch's position where Troeltsch displays similarities, amidst crucial differences, with the position of Cohen already set out.

There is no single work of Troeltsch in which he develops, as a systematic project, a theory of society. There is no single work in which Troeltsch offers a fully developed major constructive treatment of the unity of culture and the interrelation of its various elements. Thus in Troeltsch's authorship, for example, there is no single work directly comparable to Cohen's "Concept of Religion" with its theory of the unity of cultural consciousness. Much of what Troeltsch has to say on these issues is said by way of incidental comment in the process of his extensive interpretation of the Christian ethos and in his exposition of "the logical problem of the philosophy of history" in *Der Historismus und seine Probleme* (1922b). (The latter investigation is carried out in two phases: through the device of critical appraisals of various modern proposals for establishing the standards of judgment in historical matters, and the relation of such standards to a "present-day ideal of culture" and through the device of critical appraisals of various modern conceptions of the concept of historical development and of universal history.)

In fact, my own observations might well be viewed as a suggestion for reading within a single universe of discourse two works of Troeltsch's that are often regarded as disparate and disconnected: the major work of the early part of the second decade of the twentieth century, *Die Soziallehren der Christlichen Kirchen und Gruppen* (Troeltsch, 1922d; E.T. 1931); and the major project of the twenties, the massive first volume of a never fully realized work projected for two volumes, *Der Historismus und seine Probleme* (1922b). The matters I now pass in review in this chapter are also referred to by Troeltsch in more occasional essays both in the earlier periods of his authorship and in essays from the last period. This latter documentation includes the essays initially published principally during the First World War and collected in *Deutscher Geist und Westeuropa: Gesammelte kulturphilosophische Aufsaetze und Reden* (1925d), and the brief commentaries on contemporary social problems in post-World War I Europe collected in *Spektator-Briefe: Aufsaetze ueber die deutsche Revolution und die Weltpolitik 1918/22*. I claim a primary command only of the essays in *Deutscher Geist und Westeuropa*, although I will employ one representative sample from the *Spektator-Briefe*.

Not surprisingly, the appraisal of Troeltsch's performance as a theorist of society and culture has fluctuated with varying estimates of Troeltsch's views as a whole. A generation of historians of Christian theology which dismisses Troeltsch as the last epigone of *Kulturprotestantismus* will not be much interested in the details of Troeltsch's theory of society and culture. But a new generation of scholars like Wilhelm Kasch, carefully reconstructing *Die Sozialphilosophie von Ernst Troeltsch* (1963), creates a climate in which these matters can be carefully appraised. Further, Troeltsch is regarded as a significant figure by a new generation of historians of pre-1933 German political philosophy like Hermann Luebbe in his *Politische Philosophie in Deutschland: Studien zu ihrer Geschichte* (1963), and Gustav Schmidt in his *Deutscher Historismus und der Uebergang zur parlamentarischen Demokratie: Untersuchungen zu den politischen Gedanken von Meinecke, Troeltsch, Max Weber* (1964).

This rather extensive rehabilitation of Troeltsch's reputation as a theorist of society and culture, however, can be seen from yet another instructive angle. It is an angle which permits a view that does not necessarily lead to an entirely favorable estimate of Troeltsch. I refer to Uriel Tal's important studies "Liberal Protestantism and the Jews in the Second Reich, 1870-1914" (1964); and *Christians and Jews in Germany: Religion, Politics and Ideology in the Second Reich, 1870-1914* (1975). Tal is deeply informed about the politically Liberal aspects of Troeltsch's thought which interest a Luebbe and a Schmidt. Tal certainly entertains no Barthian neo-Orthodox animus against Troeltsch as a "culture Protestant"; indeed, Tal is quite aware of the major features of Troeltsch's thought which are the objects of Kasch's essay in rehabilitation. But Tal's distinctive contribution is to present, in connection with his exposition of Troeltsch, evidence of critical reactions to Troeltsch, in Troeltsch's own time, by the spokesmen of German Reform Jewish public opinion concerned with defending the cause of Germany's Jewish citizens. These German Jewish spokesmen had entertained high hopes for the development of ethical monotheism. They had expected an increasing convergence of the common elements in the Judaic and Christian traditions and a sloughing off of the particularities of Judaic legal observance and Christian Christological dogma.

These spokesmen are the popular representatives of a generation of which Hermann Cohen is the classic and culminating intellectual representative. These spokesmen, as Tal shows, are disturbed by Troeltsch's abandonment of a neo-Kantianism in the style of Cohen's companion, the theologian Wilhelm Herrmann. They are disturbed, as is Cohen, by Troeltsch's tendency to link values and truths to the historical situation in which they emerge rather than simply to assert timeless moral and religious truths. To point in a more technical direction, they are agitated by Troeltsch supplementing his neo-Kantianism with a Hegelian interest in an objective sphere in which values are instantiated in structures and institutions (Hegel's *Sittlichkeit*). These spokesmen sense that that sphere of *Sittlichkeit* Troeltsch has in view is principally the distinctively Christian civilization of the West. These spokesmen do recognize that Troeltsch is not advocating extensive institutional links between the ecclesiastical institution and the institutions of society. But Troeltsch's recommendation that the individual Christian personality bring to bear Christian values in shaping public life still looks to these spokesmen like advocacy of a culture in which Christian values play the exclusive religious role in the total unity of the culture of the German *Volk*. They see such a proposal as a threat to the status and integrity of a distinctive Jewish religious community and a blow to the hopes of late nineteenth-century German Jews for the emergence of a German society and state genuinely "neutral" on the religious issue and "pluralist" with respect to religious values in culture.

An inspection of the major current treatments of Troeltsch as a theorist of society and culture discloses then that Troeltsch is receiving a fresh appraisal from a new generation of historians of Christian thought (Kasch), from current historians of German political philosophy and German political life (Luebbe and Schmidt), and from historians of the relations of Christians and Jews in the Germany of the Second Reich (Tal). With these fresh assessments in view, I proceed to a more systematic presentation of some of Troeltsch's principal contentions.

Troeltsch is disposed to acknowledge affirmatively the irreversible secularization of many spheres of political, social, and cultural life in the modern world. As Troeltsch suggests, as early as 1906 in a prorectorial address at Heidelberg on "The Separation of Church and State" (Rubanowice, 1982:144), such spheres of life no longer appeal to the Christian belief system for an ultimate frame of meaning nor are these spheres any longer under the control of the ecclesiastical institution. In such circumstances, it is no longer appropriate for the Christian system of belief to provide directly the charter of the state nor for the warrants for political obedience to authority to be furnished directly from religious belief.

That means that in Troeltsch's Christian Liberal view of politics and culture the focus is on the individual Christian personality. As Uriel Tal has noted with such telling effect (1964; 1975), in Troeltsch's view the mature and formed Christian personality brings to bear Christian religious values in his activity in all spheres of political, social, and cultural life. Troeltsch thus re-works the classic Lutheran doctrine of the so-called secular vocation in a way that recognizes without lament or distress the genuine secularization of the modern world.

However, as Tal also points out so acutely, Troeltsch pairs these convictions about the secular calling of the Christian personality with the ad-vocacy of the notion of a *Kulturstaat*. Such a state indirectly promotes, primarily through educational means, the unitary values of the German *Volk*. A striking picture of Troeltsch's conception of those values can be seen if one inspects the semi-popular literature Troeltsch produces during the First World War in justification of the German cause. I work here from a chapter by Troeltsch on "The Spirit of German *Kultur*" in a volume on *Modern Germany in Relation to the Great War* issued in 1916 in the United States (1916). In addition to the essay by Troeltsch, this volume contains contributions by other German intellectuals such as the historian Friedrich Meinecke, and it was clearly issued in its English language edition at a time when there was still hope of securing American "neutrality" in the conflict. Interestingly enough, this volume published in the United States contains what I judge to be a full translation of an extended original German essay by Troeltsch; whereas Hans Baron, editing in 1925 a series of Troeltsch's essays on *Deutscher Geist und Westeuropa: Gesammelte kulturphilosophische Aufsaetze und Reden,* sees fit to reproduce only a truncated fragment of "Der metaphysische und religioese Geist der deutscher Kultur" (Troeltsch, 1925d:59-79).

Although Troeltsch's version of the "ideas of 1914" is sometimes marked by the extravagance of a contribution to the "culture-war," his presentation seems to be strikingly free of crude chauvinism and the glorification of power and German military might as such. Indeed, Troeltsch expresses repeatedly his anguish at the fact that the concentration, during wartime, on the survival of the particular group militates against recognizing the significance of the individual and acknowledging the claims of universal humanity which Chris-tian religion espouses. More in sorrow than in anger, Troeltsch attempts to explain the distinctiveness of German political, social, and cultural de-velopment. How and in what ways, he seems repeatedly to be asking, did

German development take so distinctive a turn, and how has Germany come to be so isolated from France, England, and America?

In a manner entirely consistent with his general interpretive method, Troeltsch insists that the present spirit of German *Kultur* not be regarded as a transcription of the only eternally valid way of ordering a modern society. (The devotees of the French revolution and French culture and even the exponents of the "rights of man" in the British and American tradition fall into that error.) Rather, the German spirit is a distinctive instance of the development of a historical reality in its individuality.

Moreover, this distinctive development of the spirit of a *Kultur* cannot be interpreted apart from developments in the economic sphere and in social class structure. (What is appropriate in interpreting the original ethos of the prophets is appropriate as well in interpreting the contemporary spirit of German *Kultur*.) In late eighteenth- and earlier nineteenth-century Germany, the classical German political ideal of the limited constitutional state as *Rechtsstaat* played a significant if not entirely dominant role. In the period between 1866 and 1871 there was a rejection of that ideal. The emergence of the state as *Machtstaat* and its justification as a *Machtstaat* is peculiarly related to the conditions of advancing industrialization and the economic situation that shaped the final Bismarckian unification of Germany under Prussian hegemony.

Troeltsch is clearly hostile to any glorification of the *Machtstaat,* and he frames a version of German war aims which disavows territorial expansion and pleads only for the right of Germany to develop distinctively in the social and cultural spheres free from the overweening tutelage of Western European ideas, whether in the French or Anglo-American version.

This vindication of the distinctive achievement of the spirit of German *Kultur* carries over into Troeltsch's way of evaluating secularization and what he calls "the separation" of church and state as institutions. Though he appraises affirmatively the secularization of many spheres of modern life and specifically advocates the "separation" of church and state, Troeltsch does not espouse the English or American conceptions of these matters. In fact, he indicates hostility to the spirit of English culture, especially as expressed by the English "middle class . . . the pillar of English trade, with its combination of strong law-abiding religiousness and keen business sense, its leaning toward the Free Church and toward an individualism that resents governmental tutelage and that expresses itself through control of government, through individual independence, and above all through public opinion" (Troeltsch, 1916:61,62).

Troeltsch is especially critical of the individualism of the British and American ethos, an individualism that sees society as an association of individuals, the state as a very limited instrument of society, and the church exclusively as a voluntary association of individuals. Troeltsch advocates, in contrast to these individualistic views of liberty, a distinctively German idea of freedom, rooted in metaphysical presuppositions best expressed in early nineteenth-century German Romanticism and the Idealistic philosophical tradition. Here the human self is seen not as an atomistic individual whose freedom is to be maximized in the face of all constraints. Rather the self is a rich and complex culture-producing being whose particular individuality takes shape in history. The inner freedom of this self can be correlated with a recognition of social order, even an organic view of society. In a culture espousing such a view of society, it is not surprising that the Bismarckian use of power in effecting German unification took without strain the form of a "state-socialism" in modern industrial society.

Understanding these assumptions about the distinctive German idea of freedom makes possible a fuller appraisal of Troeltsch's advocacy of a *Kulturstaat*. Troeltsch is not hostile to the notion of a state as a limited "constitutional state" (*Rechtstaat*). (He is no doubt in 1916 rather cool to the notion of "democracy," preferring to see that notion as one way of talking about the mobilization of the masses and mass public opinion in modern states.) Rather the state has an additional function, the function of promoting indirectly the distinctive cultural spirit of a nation, primarily through educational means which shape distinctive character (the classic notion of *Bildung*).

That German national character the Troeltsch of the early twentieth century and the wartime essays wants to promote is a national character in which the Christian religious tradition is an indispensable ingredient. (In his wartime polemics, Troeltsch glances at Catholic Germany, but it is Lutheran Germany he has principally in view). In my judgment, German Jewish communal spokesmen were right at the time to judge, and Tal is right to reiterate retrospectively, that one finds here no systematic concept of religious pluralism interior to a single state and culture nor any carefully thought through notion of the contribution of Judaism to German culture. Troeltsch has a rich appreciation of the significance of Hebrew prophetism and he can carry on a respectful dialogue with Cohen, but there is no concept of a "neutral" society which encourages religious pluralism.

In my exposition thus far, Troeltsch's wartime polemics have provided the documentary evidence for Troeltsch's theory of society and culture. Troeltsch's postwar writings of the early twenties provide an instructive complement to the wartime essays. (For an informative account of the brief essays contributed to the journal *Der Kuntswart* in the early years of the Weimar Republic and collected, edited, and published by Hans Baron in 1924 after Troeltsch's death as *Spektator-Briefe: Aufsaetze ueber die deutsche Revolution und die Weltpolitik 1918/22*, see Rubanowice, 1982:113-130.) I refer here to the classic short essay on "Socialism" from *Der Kunstwart*, February, 1920,

recently translated and published with a valuable "Introduction" by Dennis
McCann (1976). Without the benefit of a full sampling of the *Spektator-
Briefe,* I nonetheless risk the judgment that this essay on "Socialism" is one
of Troeltsch's most characteristic and most significant essays. To complete the
picture of Troeltsch's views on the early Weimar period, I refer as well to
Troeltsch's striking 1922 essay, "The Ideas of Natural Law and Humanity"
(1957b). This essay ought properly to be read, I would judge, not so much as a
scholarly treatment of the announced theme, erudite and careful though it be,
but rather as an essay by a Weimar Republic German intellectual reaching out
for reconciliation with the intellectual tradition of Britain and America and
perhaps even France. If this is the proper way to construe the essay, one can
only applaud the generosity and sense of historical appropriateness that leads
Ernest Barker in 1934 to include the work in his publication of a translation of
Otto Gierke's *Natural Law and the Theory of Society, 1500-1800.*

Two fundamental social values of the modern world come under intense
scrutiny in Troeltsch's 1920 essay on "Socialism": liberty and equality.
Troeltsch insists that the modern impulse toward liberty and the modern impulse toward equality are radically distinct. The diverse logic of the two impulses has moved modern societies in quite incompatible directions. The two
impulses are by no means capable of harmonious simultaneous realization.
Nonetheless, postwar Germany must attempt to combine a version of democracy (the impulse to liberty) and "socialism" (the impulse to equality). It is in
this connection that Troeltsch observes that the impulse to liberty in its
Anglo-American forms has issued in a concept of democracy which is not
simply "revolutionary" but displays a profoundly "conservative" element. In
this assertion, Troeltsch, who in his earlier historical studies culminating in
The Social Teaching of the Christian Churches (1931) had come to a mature
intellectual appreciation of how the ethos of Calvinism and the sects had
shaped the modern world, is now reaching out to include within the rationale of
the Weimar Republic the positive insights of the Anglo-American tradition of
political liberty.

Further, Troeltsch argues, postwar Germany must also recognize the just
protests of the industrial workers against the maldistribution of social power in
the modern industrial system. The industrial masses' full participation in the
mobilization of the war effort make it impossible to deny the industrial masses
full participation in social power in the new postwar society. A postwar
Germany must be, in some sense, socialist. But this socialism will appropriately be a "socialism of organization," a socialism of the planning of
society. Such a socialism is, in important respects, in continuity with what
Troeltsch calls the "state-socialism" of the Bismarckian *Reich.* Troeltsch rejects the radically egalitarian socialism of Leninism which is willing to make
such brutal use of state-power for the time being in the interests of an ultimate

society of individuals in a world in which state-power has disappeared.

Thus in the essay on "Socialism" Troeltsch comes to terms anew with the traditions of Anglo-American and French "civilizations" and with the challenge of Marxism in modern industrial society. In a parallel fashion, the Troeltsch of "The Idea of Natural Law and Humanity" reaches out beyond the bounds of his wartime apologies on behalf of the distinctive spirit of German *Kultur*. There is in Western civilization, Troeltsch asserts, a classic tradition, a tradition about the universally recognizable dignity of the individual, a dignity grounded in the claim that in each individual is to be found a common element of human reason. In Greek and especially in Roman Stoicism, this notion of individual dignity is supported by a pantheistic metaphysic which asserts that a divine principle of reason pervades the whole of nature. This tradition is taken over into the Christian social ethic by the Greek Fathers and Augustine and given a grounding in a theistic doctrine of creation, particularly in the doctrine of man's original created state. This doctrine is reexpressed in nineteenth and twentieth-century Catholic Thomist theory of natural law. (Here Troeltsch reaches out to Roman Catholicism in Germany and to the official teaching of the universal *magisterium*.) This doctrine in a more secularized rather than strictly Christian theological form played a role in the common culture of early modern Europe before the splits between English, French, and German developments became so pronounced. In its more secularized form this doctrine is also present in the Anglo-American and French political traditions. It is time, Troeltsch suggests, for German intellectuals once again to take the doctrine seriously and to recognize especially the claims on behalf of universal humanity which it enshrines. Such a recognition of the claims of universal humanity is a proper antidote to exclusive attention to the particularity of the German spirit and to the emphasis on the positive-historical development of cultures in their individuality.

These fresh initiatives by Troeltsch, the Weimar Republic intellectual, are in line with preoccupations expressed in the more technical work Troeltsch is simultaneously producing in the twenties, *Der Historismus und seine Probleme*. One aspect of these preoccupations is formulated within the technical sphere of the "formal logic of the philosophy of history" in *Der Historismus*, in terms of the exploration of the "standard of judgment in historical matters and its relation to present ideal of culture." More broadly, Troeltsch is constantly interested in how the past can be scrutinized for social values that can be productively integrated into a new cultural synthesis. The other aspect of these preoccupations is formulated within the technical sphere of the "formal logic of the philosophy of history," in terms of exploration of the "concept of historical development in relation to universal history." More broadly, Troeltsch is constantly concerned with the tension between historical individuality and the notion of universal human history.

In the specific way in which the notion of universal human history functions in Troeltsch's thought and in the way Troeltsch expresses the tension between the notion of universal humanity and the historical particularity of culture, Troeltsch offers an instructive contrast to Cohen. For Cohen the notion of universal history, coordinated with the notion of the one God, is a constitutive principle of his theory of society and culture. Cohen appears to have not the slightest hesitation in invoking this notion of a universal history of mankind. Of course, in connection with the present and future developments of that history, the ideal of the messianic unity of mankind is to be brought to bear in criticism of all actual societies. Nonetheless, Cohen assumes a unidirectional development in universal history and he is inattentive to the problem of the plurality of cultures in the world.

Troeltsch, on the other hand, is constantly aware of a tension between historically particular cultural traditions and the notion of humanity as such. Certainly, in the final phase of his authorship, Troeltsch, as I have indicated, strives for a new and more inclusive cultural synthesis in the West. He devotes considerable attention to the role that a Christian prophetic ethical monotheism can play in such a synthesis. To forge such a synthesis requires risk-taking with a sense of historical responsibility, and these risks are eminently worth taking. But there will always be, Troeltsch implies, a tentative quality in each new synthesis.

Moreover, precisely as he is resolutely engaged in taking the risks of proposing the terms of a new cultural synthesis in the West after World War I, Troeltsch is acutely aware that he is speaking within the situation of the "European culture-circle." There are other religio-cultural proposals looming on the horizon as possible points of orientation and organization for human cultures—especially the Asian religious traditions.

Thus Cohen invokes the notion of universal history as a constitutive principle; Troeltsch, while acknowledging the presence of the notion of universal humanity, is nonetheless continuously occupied with historical individuality.

A further instructive contrast between Cohen and Troeltsch is provided by comparing the way the idea of the one God functions in their respective theories of society and culture. As I have argued, the idea of the one God, correlated with the idea of the unity of mankind in a single history, is for Cohen a constitutive principle in his theory of culture and society. For Troeltsch the notion of the one transcendent God provides critical leverage in appraising the tradition of Christendom and societies within Western civilization. Hermann Luebbe in *Politische Philosophie in Deutschland* shrewdly titles one section of his treatment of Troeltsch "Troeltsch's historical relativizing of the essence of German *Kultur* " (1963:227-232). This historical relativizing shapes and controls the fashion in which Troeltsch advocates the "ideas of 1914." It also informs his sense for a new "cultural synthesis." But correlated with this historical relativizing is a reinforcing prophetic critical monotheistic reservation. What Troeltsch calls in his historical description of the prophets a prophetic "relative indifference to culture" now translates into this systematic prophetic critical monotheistic reservation. Only the one God, and no finite creaturely reality, is worthy of ultimate devotion.

Conclusion

Without doubt, Cohen and Troeltsch are utterly typical of the cultural time and place in which they work. Both assume that neo-Kantian and neo-Hegelian conceptualities are the great alternative options for Western intellectuals. Both assume that their respective religious traditions must be radically reconstructed if those traditions are to be judged credible in the modern world. Both assume that Western civilization has a future as well as a past, though Troeltsch is more impressed than Cohen by the culturally conditioned character of the "European culture-circle."

But Cohen and Troeltsch also move against the stream. Neither succumbs to that poisonous cultural pessimism so prevalent among many turn-of-the-century German and French intellectuals. Neither is disposed to agree with Nietzsche in declaring the bankruptcy of the received religious and moral traditions of the West. Neither is disposed to find with Weber in discerning in the present scene only an anarchic plurality of conflicting cultural values.

Both Cohen and Troeltsch retain a sense of the vigor and health of man's moral awareness and a confidence that monotheistic religion can structure and reinforce that moral consciousness. They are confident as well that efforts for the construction of a modern culture can come to a successful outcome.

Whether with respect to the typical or the idiosyncratic features of their thought, the work of both Cohen and Troeltsch meets a barrage of criticism in the generation after their own. Cohen, say some of his Judaic critics, is too rationalistic and too confident about the robustness of the moral consciousness; Cohen, such critics insist, is properly superseded by the existential-ontological system of Franz Rosenzweig and the existential-expressivist thought of Martin Buber. Cohen, say others of his Jewish critics, is deluded about German-Jewish symbiosis and about the prospects of Judaism as a base for modern Western culture. The German Jewish dialogue, a critic like Scholem insists, was never a proper dialogue, only pathetic Jewish monologue. The illusion of a German-Jewish symbiosis concealed from the European Jewish community their peril and contributed to the community's ultimate destruction. After the Holocaust such ways of thinking are at best historical curiosities if they are not downright malign in impact. Cohen's Zionist critics, Scholem contends, were right.

Troeltsch, say his neoorthodox critics in the next generation, is the last major representative of culture-Protestantism. He imperils the uniqueness of Christian revelation by correlating the Christian pattern of faith and life with dominant trends of modern secular culture. His theological work in the *Glaubenslehre* is mere dilettantism. His efforts at theological reconstruction founder on the problem of historicism.

In my judgment, devotion to such stereotypical views of Cohen and Troeltsch blocks adequate historical reconstruction of their intellectual programs. Acquiescence in such dismissal of the significance of Cohen and Troeltsch makes impossible an adequate appraisal of their accomplishments.

This monograph is an essay in historical investigation and the recovery of complex patterns of thought beyond such stereotypes. It seeks, further, to be an essay in rehabilitation.

The broadest claim here argued is that, despite the disrepute in which the notion is still held currently in theologically sophisticated circles, ethical monotheism is one of the great alternative options for the modern reconstruction of both the Judaic and Christian traditions. Admittedly, to construe Judaism as ethical monotheism is to read the classic tradition of Rabbinic Judaism from the second century to the eighteenth in a very selective and partial way—a way that gives normative significance to the prophetic faith and ethos an an unsurpassable moment in Judaic religion. And it is more than likely that construing Judaism as ethical monotheism involves and will continue to involve an appropriation of the Kantian philosophical conceptuality for expressing Judaic belief and ethical teaching.

But, it would appear, even after the Holocaust and the normalization of Jewish life in Israel, Jewish life endures in a Western Diaspora, principally in the United States, Canada, and France. In such a situation, can one simply dismiss as outmoded the hard conceptual core of Cohen's position—the notion of the Jewish people as an ethnic-religious minority providing for the total culture the distinctive ideas of the one God, unitary human history, and a goal of messianic humanity? In such a situation, is it totally without validity to construe Judaism as a social ethic and to reflect on the interaction of Judaic and Christian religious elements in the increasingly secularized culture of the West?

It is not entirely fashionable at present to interpret Christianity as ethical monotheism. But once again, I would contend that the notion provides one of the major alternative options for modern reconstruction of Christian belief. Troeltsch's proposal indicates that such a reading of Christianity need not be exclusively tied to a Kantian view of the moral consciousness. Neo-Hegelian awareness of the relation of beliefs and mores to historical situations and neo-Hegelian interest in the spheres of values instantiated in the patterns of institutions can also form a part of an ethical monotheistic reading of Christianity. Such neo-Hegelian themes and procedures provide resources for thinking about Christianity as a social ethic in a modern world in process of secularization. What is more, to interpret Christian ethical monotheism, with

Troeltsch, in the light of the "prophetic principle" provides critical leverage against all forms of idolatry including the idolatries of Christendom.

Further, if I read correctly the current discussion in moral philosophy, the late nineteenth-century debate between neo-Kantians and neo-Hegelians is by no means a simple historical curiosity. Indeed, major attention is being paid once again to the Kantian interest in moral claims universally valid across cultural boundaries; and, simultaneously, major attention is being paid once again to the contrasting Hegelian interest in the particularities of the total ethos of an individual society and culture.

I have not sought in this monograph to provide an entirely new interpretation of Cohen. Rather, I have drawn together a number of disparate aspects of current Cohen-interpretation to show, from a particular perspective, their interconnection: especially Cohen's presentation of Judaism as a religion of reason drawn by "idealization" from Judaic sources; Cohen's interpretation of the prophetic faith and ethos; Cohen's presentation of Judaism as a social ethic for an emancipatory society; and Cohen's interest in the unity of the cultural consciousness. I have deliberately tried to report and assess the state of the question in various areas of current Cohen scholarship; and I have not hesitated to rely extensively on such particularly instructive informants as Guenther and Schwarzschild. I do believe that putting the whole picture together in this way contributes to a fresh understanding of Cohen and permits me on such particular topics as the unity of cultural consciousness to break fresh ground.

I have not sought in this monograph to provide an entirely fresh interpretation of Troeltsch. I hope that those who are already caught up in the Troeltsch revival will find what I have to say about Troeltsch's controversies with Cohen both novel and unexpected. I hope as well that I have provided some new indications of the theological importance of Troeltsch's *Glaubenslehre.* Can I dare to hope that what I have to say about Troeltsch, the interpreter of the spirit of German *Kultur* and the envisioner of a new cultural synthesis in the West, will be carefully examined and not simply dismissed as further evidence for a damning indictment of *Kulturprotestantismus?*

I have been concerned, in recent years, to promote the development of a descriptive discipline called "comparative theology: Judaic and Christian." Such a discipline deals with the major highly articulated systems of Judaic and Christian thought. Insofar as it treats modern systems of Judaic and Christian thought, such a discipline also deals with how such systems employ such modern philosophical conceptualities as the Kantian and Hegelian.

A comparison can be especially informative when a Judaic and a Christian thinker and system of thought have to some extent a common agenda. The inquiry is even more informative when two thinkers have each other's work directly in view. If they engage in significant controversy, so much the better.

This monograph on "Cohen and Troeltsch: Ethical Monotheistic Religion and Theory of Culture" is offered then as an exercise in comparative theology: Judaic and Christian.

Works Consulted

Altmann, Alexander

    1962   "Hermann Cohens Begriff der Korrelation." *In Zwei Welten: Siegfried Moses zum Fuenfundsiebzigsten Geburtstag,* ed. Hans Tramer. Tel Aviv: Verlag Bitaon. Pp. 366-399.

Anchor, Robert

    1967   "Rickert, Heinrich." *Encyclopedia of Philosophy,* ed. Paul Edwards, ed. Vol. 7. New York: Macmillan. Pp. 192-194.

Beck, Lewis White

    1967   "Neo-Kantianism." *Encyclopedia of Philosophy,* ed. Paul Edwards. Vol. 5. New York: Macmillan. Pp. 469-473.

Berger, Peter L.

    1963   "Charisma and Religious Innovation: The Social Location of Israelite Prophecy." *American Sociological Review* 28: 940-950.

Cassirer, Ernst

    1943   "Hermann Cohen, 1842-1918." *Social Research* 10:219-232.

    1944   "Judaism and the Modern Political Myths." *Contemporary Jewish Record* 7:115-126.

Clements, Ronald E.

    1976   *One Hundred Years of Old Testament Interpretation.* Philadelphia: Westminster Press.

Cohen, Hermann

    1907   "Religion und Sittlichkeit." *Hermann Cohens Juedische Schriften.* Band 3. *Zur juedischen Religionsphilosophie und ihrer Geschichte,* ed. Bruno Strauss. Berlin: C. A. Schwetschke, 1924. Pp. 98-168.

1913a   "Die Eigenart der alttestamentlichen Religion." *Hermann Cohens Juedische Schriften*. Band 2. *Zur juedischen Zeitgeschichte*, ed. Bruno Strauss. Berlin: C. A. Schwetschke, 1924. Pp. 410-415.

1913b   "Zwei Rektoratsreden an der Berliner Universitaet." *Hermann Cohens Juedische Schriften*. Band 2. *Zur juedischen Zeitgeschichte*, ed. Bruno Strauss. Berlin: C. A. Schwetschke, 1924. Pp. 404-409.

1914   "Ueber das Eigentuemliche des deutschen Geistes." *Philosophische Vortraege veroeffentlicht von der Kantgesellschaft*. Nr. 8. Berlin: Ruether und Reichard (also reprinted in *Hermann Cohens Schriften zur Philosophie und Zeitgeschichte*. Band 1. [Albert Goerland and Ernst Cassirer, eds.]). Berlin: Akademie Verlag, 1928. Pp. 527-570.

1915   *Der Begriff der Religion im System der Philosophie*. Giessen: Alfred Toepelmann.

1916a   "Das soziale Ideal bei Platon und den Propheten." *Hermann Cohens Juedische Schriften*. Band 1. *Ethische und religioese Grundfragen*. Berlin: C. A. Schwetschke. 1924. Pp. 306-330.

1916b   "Religion und Zionismus." *Hermann Cohens Juedische Schriften*. Band 2. *Zur juedischen Zeitgeschichte*, ed. Bruno Strauss. Berlin: C. A. Schwetschke, 1924. Pp. 319-327.

1916c   "Antwort auf das offene Schreiben des Herrn Dr. Martin Buber an Hermann Cohen." *Hermann Cohens Juedische Schriften*. Band 2. *Zur juedischen Zeitgeschichte*. Berlin: C. A. Schwetschke, 1924. Pp. 328-341.

1916d   "Die ethischen und die historischen Motive der Religion." *Hermann Cohens Juedische Schriften*. Band 3. *Zur juedischen Religionsphilosophie und ihrer Geschichte*, ed. Bruno Strauss. Berlin: C. A. Schwetschke, 1924. Pp. 197-202.

1916e   "Emanzipation." [1912] *Hermann Cohens Juedische Schriften*. Band 2. *Zur juedischen Zeitgeschichte*. Berlin: C. A. Schwetschke, 1924. Pp. 220-228.

1916f   "Der Jude in der christlichen Kultur." *Hermann Cohens Juedische Schriften.* Band 2. *Zur juedischen Zeitgeschichte.* Berlin: C. A. Schwetschke, 1924. Pp. 193-209.

1917a   "Der Prophetismus und die Soziologie." *Hermann Cohens Juedische Schriften.* Band 2. *Zur juedischen Zeitgeschichte,* ed. Bruno Strauss. Berlin: C. A. Schwetschke, 1924. Pp. 398-401.

1917b   "Graetzens Philosophie der juedischen Geschichte." *Hermann Cohens Juedische Schriften.* Band 3. *Zur juedischen Religionsphilosophie und ihrer Geschichte.* Berlin: C. A. Schwetschke, 1924. Pp. 203-212.

1918   "Julius Wellhausen." *Hermann Cohens Juedische Schriften.* Band 2. *Zur juedischen Zeitgeschichte,* ed. Bruno Strauss. Berlin: C. A. Schwetschke, 1924. Pp. 463-468.

1921   *Ethik des Reinen Willens.* Dritte Auflage. [First edition of this work, 1904]. Berlin: Bruno Cassirer.

1929   *Religion der Vernunft aus den Quellen des Judentums.* Zweite Auflage. Frankfurt am Main: J. Kauffmann.

1972   *Religion of Reason out of the Sources of Judaism,* trans. with an "Introduction" by Simon Kaplan. New York: Frederick Ungar.

Drescher, Hans-Georg

1976   "Ernst Troeltsch's Intellectual Development." *Ernst Troeltsch and the Future of Theology,* ed. John Powell Clayton. Cambridge: Cambridge University Press. Pp. 3-32.

Frei, Hans W.

1965   "Niebuhr's Theological Background." *Faith and Ethics: The Theology of H. Richard Niebuhr,* ed. Paul Ramsey. New York: Harper and Row. Pp. 9-64.

Gerrish, Brian A.

1975   "Jesus, Myth and History: Troeltsch's Stand in the 'Christ-Myth' Debate." *Journal of Religion* 55:13-35.

1976   "Ernst Troeltsch and the Possibility of a Systematic The-
            ology." *Ernst Troeltsch and the Future of Theology*, ed. John
            Powell Clayton. Cambridge: Cambridge University Press.
            Pp. 100-135.

Gottwald, Norman K.

1964   *All the Kingdoms of the Earth: Israelite Prophecy and
            International Relations in the Ancient Near East.* New York:
            Harper and Row.

Guenther, Henning

1972   *Philosophie des Fortschritts: Hermann Cohens Recht-
            fertigung der buergerlichen Gesellschaft.* Muenchen: Wilhelm
            Goldmann.

Hahn, Herbert F.

1954   *Old Testament in Modern Research.* Philadelphia:
            Muhlenberg Press.

1959   "Wellhausen's Interpretation of Israel's Religious History."
            Essays in Jewish Life and Thought, ed. Joseph Blau. New
            York: Columbia University Press.

Kasch, Wilhelm F.

1963   *Die Sozialphilosophie von Ernst Troeltsch.* Tuebingen: J. C.
            B. Mohr (Paul Siebeck).

Klatzkin, Jacob

1980a   "Germanism and Judaism: A Critique." *The Jew: Essays
            from Martin Buber's Journal: Der Jude 1916-1928*, ed.
            Arthur Cohen. University: University of Alabama Press. Pp.
            64-84.

1980b   "Hermann Cohen." *The Jew: Essays from Martin Buber's
            Journal: Der Jude, 1916-1928*, ed. Arthur Cohen.
            University: University of Alabama Press. Pp. 251-261.

Kraeling, Emil

1955   *The Old Testament since the Reformation.* London:
            Lutterworth Press.

Kraus, Hans-Joachim

  1969   *Geschichte der historisch-kritischen Erforschung des Alten Testament.* (Zweite Auflage. Neukirchen-Vluyn) Neukirchener Verlag.

  1970   *Die Biblische Theologie: Ihre Geschichte und Problematik.* Neukirchen-Vluyn Neukirchener Verlag.

Liebeschuetz, Hans

  1960   "Max Wiener's Reinterpretation of Liberal Judaism." *Leo Baeck Institute, Year Book* 5:35-57.

Little, H. Ganse

  1968   "Ernst Troeltsch on History, Decision and Responsibility." *Journal of Religion* 48:205-234.

Luebbe, Hermann

  1963   *Politische Philosophie in Deutschland: Studien zu ihrer Geschichte.* Basel: Benno Schwabe.

  1965   *Saekularisierung: Geschichte eines ideenpolitischen Begriffs.* Freiburg/Muenchen: Verlag Karl Alber.

Mandelbaum, Maurice

  1938   *The Problem of Historical Knowledge: An Answer to Relativism.* New York: Liveright.

Mosse, George L.

  1970   "Left-Wing Intellectuals in the Weimar Republic." *Germans and Jews: The Right, the Left and the Search for a "Third Force" in Pre-Nazi Germany.* New York: Grosset and Dunlap. Pp. 171-228.

Niebuhr, H. Richard

  1951   *Christ and Culture.* New York: Harper and Bros.

Pulzer, Peter

  1979   "Jewish Participation in Wilhelmine Politics." *Jews and Germans from 1860-1933: The Problematic Symbiosis,* ed. David Bronson. Heidelberg: Carl Winter. Pp. 78-99.

  1980   "Why Was There a Jewish Question in Imperial Germany?" *Year Book, Leo Baeck Institute,* 25: 133-146.

Rubanowice, Robert J.

1982   *Crisis in Consciousness: The Thought of Ernst Troeltsch.*
                Tallahassee: University Presses of Florida.

Rupp, George

1977   *Culture-Protestantism: German Liberal Theology at the Turn
                of the Twentieth Century.* Missoula, Mont.: Scholars Press.

Sarna, Nahum M.

1975   "Abraham Geiger and Biblical Scholarship." *New Perspec-
                tives on Abraham Geiger: An HUC-JIR Symposium,* ed.
                Jacob Petuchowski. New York: KTAV. Pp. 17-30.

Schmidt, Gustav

1964   *Deutscher Historismus und der Uebergang zur parla-
                mentarischen Demokratie: Untersuchungen zu den politi-
                schen Gedanken von Meinecke, Troeltsch, Max Weber. His-
                torische Studien.* Heft 389. Luebeck and Hamburg:
                Matthiesen Verlag.

Schwarzschild, Steven S.

1975   "The Tenability of Hermann Cohen's Construction of the
                Self." *Journal of the History of Philosophy* 13:361-384.

1979   "'Germanism and Judaism'—Hermann Cohen's Normative
                Paradigm of the German-Jewish Symbiosis." *Jews and
                Germans from 1860-1933: The Problematic Symbiosis,* ed.
                David Bronson. Heidelberg: Carl Winter. Pp. 129-172.

1981   "Introduction," Hermann Cohen. *Ethik des reinen Willens.*
                Funft Auflage, *Werke,* ed. Helmut Holzhey. Hildesheim:
                Georg Olms. Pp. vii-xxxvii.

Schweid, Eliezer

1983   "Summary: Hermann Cohen as a Biblical Exegete." *Daat: A
                Journal of Jewish Philosophy and Kabbalah,* no. 10
                (Winter): 52.

Tal, Uriel

1964   "Liberal Protestantism and the Jews in the Second Reich,
                1870-1914." *Jewish Social Studies* 26:23-41.

1975   *Christians and Jews in Germany: Religion, Politics and Ideology in the Second Reich, 1870-1914.* Ithaca: Cornell University Press.

1980   "Changing Approaches to Society in Nineteenth Century Jewish Thought." Inauguration of the Jacob and Shoshana Schreiber Fellowship in the History of Contemporary Judaism, Oxford Center for Postgraduate Studies and Tel Aviv University. Pp. 27-42.

1982   "Law and Theology: On the Status of German Jewry at the Outset of the Third Reich (1933/4)." Third Annual Lecture of the Jacob M. and Shoshana Schreiber Chair of Contemporary Jewish History, Tel Aviv University, Faculty of Humanities. Pp. 3-33.

Troeltsch, Ernst

1912   "Contingency." *Encycolpedia of Religion and Ethics,* ed. James Hastings. Vol. 4. New York: Charles Scribners. Pp. 87-89.

1915   Review of "Hermann Cohen, *Die religioesen Bewegungen der Gegenwart: Ein Vortrag." Theologische Literaturzeitung* 40, Nr. 16/17: cols. 383-386.

1916   "The Spirit of German Kultur." *Modern Germany in Relation to the Great War,* by various German Writers, trans. William Wallace Whitelock. New York: Mitchell Kennerley. Pp. 56-88.

1918   Review of "Hermann Cohen, *Der Begriff der Religion im System der Philosophie." Theologische Literaturzeitung* 43, Nr. 4/5: cols. 57-62.

1922a   "Grundprobleme der Ethik." [1902] *Zur religioesen Lage, Religionsphilosophie und Ethik, Gesammelte Schriften.* Band 2. Zweite Auflage, ed. Hans Baron. Tuebingen: J. C. B. Mohr. Pp. 552-672.

1922b   *Der Historismus und seine Probleme. Gesammelte Schriften,* Band 3. Tuebingen: J. C. B. Mohr.

1922c   "Was heisst 'Wesen des Christentums'?" [1912] *Zur religioesen Lage, Religionsphilosophie und Ethik, Gesammelte Schriften.* Band 2. Zweite Auflage, ed. Hans Baron. Tuebingen: J. C. B. Mohr. Pp. 386-451.

1922d   *Die Soziallehren der Christlichen Kirchen und Gruppen, Gesammelte Schriften.* Band 3. Tuebingen: J. C. B. Mohr.

1925a   *"Glaube und Ethos der hebraeischen Propheten."* [1916] *Aufsaetze zur Geistesgeschichte und Religionssoziologie, Gesammelte Schriften,* Band 4, ed. Hans Baron. Tuebingen: J. C. B. Mohr. Pp. 34-64, 820, 821.

1925b   "Die alte Kirche." [1916/1917] *Aufsaetze zur Geistesgeschichte und Religionssoziologie, Gesammelte Schriften.* Band 4, ed. Hans Baron. Tuebingen: J. C. B. Mohr. Pp. 65-121.

1925c   *Glaubenslehre.* Muenchen: Duncker and Humblot.

1925d   *Deutscher Geist und Westeuropa: Gesammelte kultur-philosophische Aufsaetze und Reden,* ed. Hans Baron. Tuebingen: J. C. B. Mohr (Paul Siebeck).

1931   *The Social Teaching of the Christian Churches* (translated by Olive Wyon). 2 vols. London: George Allen and Unwin.

1957a   *Christian Thought: Its History and Application.* [1923] New York: Meridian.

1957b   "The Ideas of Natural Law and Humanity." [1922] In Otto Gierke, *Natural Law and Theory of Society: 1500-1800,* trans. with an "Introduction" by Ernest Barker. Boston: Beacon Press. Pp. 201-222.

1968   "Translation of 'Grundprobleme der Ethik,'" with introduction by Donald E. Miller. *The Shaping of Modern Christian Thought* by Warren F. Groff and Donald E. Miller. Cleveland and New York: World Publishing Company. Pp. 226-244.

1976   "Ernst Troeltsch's Essay on 'Socialism,'" translated with an "Introduction" by Dennis F. McCann, *Journal of Religious Ethics* 4: 159-180.

1977   "What Does 'Essence of Christianity' Mean?" *Ernst Troeltsch: Writings on Theology and Religion*, trans. and ed. Robert Morgan and Michael Pye. Atlanta: John Knox Press. Pp. 124-179.

Weber, Max

1952   *Ancient Judaism*, trans. and ed. Hans H. Gerth and Don Martindale. New York: Free Press.

Wiener, Max

1947   "The Conception of Mission in Traditional and Modern Judaism." *YIVO Annual of Jewish Social Science* 2: 9-24.

Willey, Thomas E.

1978   *Back to Kant: The Revival of Kantianism in German Social and Historical Thought, 1860-1914.* Detroit: Wayne State University Press.

Wilson, Robert R.

1980   *Prophecy and Society in Ancient Israel.* Philadelphia: Fortress Press.

Wyman, Walter E., Jr.

1983   *The Concept of "Glaubenslehre": Ernst Troeltsch and the Theological Heritage of Schleiermacher.* Chico, Calif.: Scholars Press.

Index of Names

Index of Topics

BROWN JUDAIC STUDIES SERIES

Continued from back cover